THE JOY OF MISERY

T0353297

David Pinner

THE JOY OF MISERY

Four One-Act Plays

OBERON BOOKS
LONDON

WWW.OBERONBOOKS.COM

This collection first published in 2012 by Oberon Books Ltd
521 Caledonian Road, London N7 9RH
Tel: +44 (0) 20 7607 3637 / Fax: +44 (0) 20 7607 3629
e-mail: info@oberonbooks.com
www.oberonbooks.com

A catalogue record for this book is available from the British Library.

PB ISBN: 978-1-84943-385-3
Digital ISBN: 978-1-84943-632-8

Cover design by James Illman

Visit www.oberonbooks.com to read more about all our books
and to buy them. You will also find features, author interviews and
news of any author events, and you can sign up for e-newsletters
so that you're always first to hear about our new releases.

Contents

Foreword

I have written five one-act-plays, and four of them are in this volume. The fifth, *Edred, the Vampyre* is in my Vampire Trilogy. *Cartoon, An Evening With The G.L.C.* and *Shakebag* were all written for the Soho Poly, and they were performed there in the mid-1970s. Whereas I wrote *Succubus* in 2011 to accompany *Edred, the Vampyre.*

My first one-act play, *Cartoon,* which starred Linda Thorson (who took over from Diana Rigg in *The Avengers)* is a comedy about cartoons and the joy of misery. I've always been fascinated with cartoons as they work on the premise that laughter can be caused by other people's pain and distress. I focused on a quartet of characters in a pub, whose lives are linked by their disastrous histories. There is Siegfried, the cartoonist, who is in a home for alcoholics. As a result, he consumes three litres of grapefruit juice a day, and he is always weeping because of his continuous winning streak on a one-armed bandit. Jane, the unmarried barmaid, cheerily allows herself to give birth to a child every year, despite the chaos that ensues. Hughie, who is an ex-public schoolboy, is an enthusiastic voyeur of other people's despair. While his erstwhile girlfriend, the flaky Elaine, is perpetually bemoaning the fact that her husband has gone off with yet another of his buxom secretaries. As Siegfried, the cartoonist, remarks; 'If you cut succulent slices off people, then everyone laughs. However, if the scalpel slips, then you're down to the bone.' But then, of course, comedy can be seen as tragedy speeded up.

The genesis of *An Evening With The G.L.C.* was quite different. At the time of writing, my friend, Professor Stephen Haseler, was Chairman of the General Purposes Committee on the Greater London Council. As I have always been fascinated by politics, he gave me the low-down on what was really happening in London at the time, and some of it was hair-raising. I decided to set my play in a television studio, where the Labour Councillor Rennip, who is on the G.L.C., is invited onto a combative Current Affairs programme 'Confrontation', to defend his political record. His son, Cliff, who is in the Sixth Form, is also there to pose some very awkward questions for his father. Cliff has been secretly writing down what his father has said privately at home, which greatly differs from the Councillor's public pronouncements. The play explores public morality versus political expediency, and it exposes the dire state of London. Indeed, many of London's problems, which I examine in the play, have not improved very much in the best part of a third of a century, so the play is still sadly prescient.

My third one-act play, *Shakebag,* which was performed at the Soho Poly in 1976, is a farcical comedy about an amateur company's first rehearsal of *Macbeth* and *A Midsummer Night's Dream* on Shakespeare's birthday. The title came about because in the Elizabethan play, *Arden of Faversham,* (which is thought to have been written by Christopher Marlowe, although it is anonymous), there are two murderers by the names of Black Will and Shakebag, and this can only be a dig at Shakespeare. In *Shakebag,* there is a group of enthusiastic-but-very-self-centred amateurs, who inadvertently set about 'murdering' two of Shakespeare's finest plays. There is Christabel, the pretty twenty-year-old, with her infectious giggle and her love affair with her compact mirror. Jo, the much-put-upon school-teacher director, who can never get a word in edgeways. Beatrice, the self-proclaimed world-authority on the Bard, with a penchant for large gins. Rod, the American salesman, with his dodgy fly-zip and love of the Method. Bill, the carpenter-cum-factotum, who thinks all actors are noddies, so he plays the drums, and hammers during most of their speeches. And, finally, there is the one professional actor, Martin, who is 'only here for the beer'. And all the while the amused ghost of Shakespeare, with his birthday tankard in his hand, looks down from on high on these thespian 'mechanicals', who are the clownish 'ciphers to his great accompt'.

My fourth play is *Succubus,* which I wrote in 2011 to compliment *Edred, the Vampyre.* In *Edred,* I focus on a thousand-year-old Anglo Saxon, bisexual vampire, who 'slept with Shakespeare but never bit him', and who lived through the world created by Genghis Khan, Ivan the Terrible, Robespierre, Hitler and Stalin, so the play explores the male monsters of history. Whereas in *Succubus,* the life of the heroine, Lili, is more ambivalent. Lili may or may not have been many things, including a Mesopotamian storm demon, a thousand-year-old witch, an eternal succubus, or even the Moon Goddess Herself. The play focuses on Mark, who is an ex-alcoholic, Born Again Christian, with a burning secret that Lili reveals in a terrifying manner. The action takes place in Mark's basement, which he has turned into his chapel, with an altar as its centre piece. The play explores female myths and male fears, and it questions various beliefs, including the occult, paganism, pantheism and Christianity. The action fluctuates between comedy and horror.

David Pinner

CARTOON
A COMEDY IN ONE ACT

Characters

JANE

HUGHIE LESSOR

ELAINE NEVISON

SIEGFRIED TAYLOR

Cartoon was first performed at the Soho Poly, London on 27th March 1973 with the following cast:

JANE, Bridget Price

HUGHIE LESSOR, Andrew McCulloch

ELAINE NEVISON, Linda Thorson

SIEGFRIED TAYLOR, Derek Royle

Director, Fredrick Proud

Designer, Claire Lyth

A lounge bar in an antiquated pub, with a mixture of the old and the very new, and there is a fruit machine in the corner.

It is high summer.

HUGHIE LESSOR, in his late 30s, is stylishly dressed, and sitting at the bar.

Restlessly he pours a small quantity of beer from his glass onto the bar-top.

JANE, a voluptuous, quick-witted Lancashire barmaid, watches HUGHIE as he proceeds to play noughts and crosses in his spilt beer.

JANE: D'you have to?

HUGHIE: Hm?

JANE: Play mucky buggers with your fingers?

HUGHIE: Oh. Sorry. Was I?

> *He looks at his watch, then he peers round the bar. He notes that the only other customer is SIEGFRIED TAYLOR, who is sitting in the far corner staring at the fruit machine.*
>
> *SIEGFRIED, who looks unkempt, tousled and hasn't shaved for several days, is a thick-set man in his late 40s. In his prime he was a handsome man, but now he has a red nose from years of drinking. Although at the moment he's nursing a grapefruit juice.*

JANE: *(To HUGHIE.)* Late is she?

HUGHIE: Always. You don't have any champagne on ice, do you?

JANE: Where'd you think you are? The Hilton?

HUGHIE: Last year we couldn't even get a stool in here.

JANE: *(While she arranges a salad on the bar.)* You couldn't have come on a Monday, then. Can always get a stool on a Monday. 'Fact you can have as many as you like. As you can see.

HUGHIE: *(Grinning.)* Are you married?

JANE: No. You proposing?

Laughing HUGHIE shakes his head. Then he turns to watch SIEGFRIED, who is now playing the fruit machine. A moment later fifteen metal counters clatter out. In response SIEGFRIED yowls in pain.

JANE: Never seen a man with such a gift for oranges.

HUGHIE: What?

JANE: Sticky weather, isn't it? Very moist in the creases.

HUGHIE: Yes, well… I'll have another half, please. But just… ordinary bitter this time…

JANE pulls the beer.

JANE: 'Bout to posit a complaint, are we?

HUGHIE: No, I just hate all the fizz in the other, that's all.

JANE: *(Cheekily.)* Are you married?

HUGHIE gives her some money.

HUGHIE: Take it out of this, and have a double on me.

ELAINE LEVISON comes into the bar. She is an attractive woman in her late 30s, and she is wearing a black trouser-suit and sunglasses.

She looks round her. Then she goes over to HUGHIE, who is staring into space. Catching him off guard, ELAINE kisses him on the cheek.

ELAINE: Sorry I'm late, darling.

HUGHIE kisses her cheek.

HUGHIE: Doesn't matter, darling.

She kisses his other cheek.

ELAINE: Lovely to see you, darling.

He kisses her other cheek.

HUGHIE: And you, too, darling.

ELAINE: Best part of a year, isn't it?

HUGHIE: Yes, darling. Fancy a sandwich, a Scotch egg, or a couple of bangers, or something?

ELAINE: *(Shaking her head.)* 'Fraid it's my rabbit-food week.

HUGHIE: Hard cheese! I mean er… *(To JANE.)* Do you think you could kindly make us an appetising concoction, covering up the fact that it's low on calories? *(Pointing to a table with three chairs.)* And then would you bring it over there, please?

JANE: To hear is to obey. *(SIEGFRIED wins again on the slot machine. Then he pulls out his handkerchief and dabs his eyes with it as JANE calls over to him.)* Oranges again, luv?

HUGHIE: *(Whispering to JANE.)* Has he got Hay fever?

JANE: No, he's just crying.

HUGHIE: Really?

JANE: Yes, he always does when he wins, and for the last week he's done nothing but win. My boss says he's had to go away for a rest, 'cause it gives him indigestion.

HUGHIE: Huh?

JANE: Watching Siggy clicking all them oranges up.

ELAINE: *(To JANE.)* Yes, of course…that's Siegfried Taylor, the cartoonist, isn't it?

JANE: Yeah. How'd you know?

ELAINE crosses herself.

ELAINE: Good God! Could I have a double gin and tonic, Hughie darling?

HUGHIE kisses her on the cheek.

HUGHIE: Of course, Elaine darling.

JANE: *(To ELAINE.)* You can go to your table if you want. I'll make your gin for you.

ELAINE: You're very kind.

JANE: *(To ELAINE.)* But *you're* married, aren't you – Miss?

ELAINE sniffs tearfully.

HUGHIE: What's the matter, darling?

JANE: Hay Fever?

HUGHIE escorts ELAINE across the lounge, while SIEGFRIED wins again, and lets out another howl of despair.

HUGHIE: *(To SIEGFRIED.)* Forgive me for saying so, but you're a bloody genius!

SIEGFRIED: *(With a Yorkshire accent.)* Ay. Even amazes me.

ELAINE: *(Hesitantly.)* Hello, Siggy.

SIEGFRIED: *(Recognising her for the first time.)* Elaine! I'll come over and join you in a minute, if I may.

ELAINE: *(Uncertainly.)* Yes…that would be…very nice.

She smiles nervously at SIEGFRIED. Then she sits in the opposite corner with HUGHIE.

HUGHIE: *(Whispering to ELAINE.)* You…know him, then?

In response ELAINE clutches HUGHIE's hand tearfully.

ELAINE: So…how's your year been, Hughie?

HUGHIE: Well, it's been quite er…

ELAINE: *(Overriding him.)* Mine's been absolutely disastrous!

JANE comes over with ELAINE's double gin and tonic.

JANE: Rabbit food coming up.

They all look round as more counters gush out of the fruit machine. SIEGFRIED gives another yowl. Then he waves JANE over.

SIEGFRIED: Another grapefruit juice, Jane, God help me.

JANE nods, and goes off behind the bar.

ELAINE: *(Squeezing HUGHIE's hand.)* He's left me!

HUGHIE: Mm?

ELAINE: *(Touching her sunglasses.)* You can't see me crying with these on, can you? I mean, there's no point me wearing them if you can.

HUGHIE: You're serious, aren't you?

ELAINE: I'll take 'em off if you like. As long as you don't mind my mascara running...

HUGHIE: Of course I don't mind it running. *(She takes off her glasses.)* What I mean is…when did your husb…er Harry leave you?

ELAINE: Four weeks ago.

HUGHIE: Why didn't you give me a ring?

ELAINE: I was disconnected.

HUGHIE: Jesus!

ELAINE: We had a row over who should pay the telephone bill, so neither of us did, and he went off with a fat cow from Kensington.

HUGHIE: Typical.

ELAINE: I suppose she wasn't really fat, just…

HUGHIE: *(Salaciously)* …Extremely well-developed?

ELAINE: *(Hurt.)* Lust is a very nasty thing, Hughie, when seen in the eyes of a friend for a woman he's never even met.

HUGHIE: I'm sorry. No, really.

ELAINE: And she's younger than me. But she dyes her hair, though. Platinum blonde. And I'm pretty sure that they're not all her own teeth, either.

HUGHIE: Now don't upset yourself, love.

ELAINE: But she walks like someone who is very…fecund. You know that kind of fecund walk, when even the shoulders and boobs move like the hips.

More counters clatter out of the fruit machine. Cursing, SIEGFRIED pummels the machine.

SIEGFRIED: I can't bear it, I can't bloody bear it!

JANE reappears with a very large tray, on which are two salads and the fruit juice. She passes the juice to SIEGFRIED.

JANE: Perhaps this'll help, luv. *(Then she plonks the two salads on the table in front of ELAINE and HUGHIE.)* D'you want French dressing or the House?

HUGHIE: *(To JANE, about SIEGFRIED, who is yowling again.)* What the hell's the matter with him?

JANE: Life. So which dressing d'you want?

They watch SIEGFRIED, who is now slumped on his knees, staring at the fruit machine as more counters spatter onto the carpet.

HUGHIE: French, please.

ELAINE: I certainly don't want the House! 'Fact I don't want any dressing at all, thank you.

JANE goes off while SIEGFRIED picks up his loot. ELAINE toys with her salad.

HUGHIE: So, Elaine, are you a getting a divor…? I mean, are you taking legal action?

ELAINE: *(Bursting into tears.)* No, *he* is!

HUGHIE: Hm?!

ELAINE: I was unfaithful first!

HUGHIE: What?

ELAINE: But only once. With Tom.

HUGHIE: Tom?

ELAINE: His brother. After I beat him at Canasta. It was the least I could do.

JANE comes back with some mayonnaise.

JANE: Sorry, I've just remembered. We haven't got French or House dressing today.

HUGHIE: Doesn't matter.

JANE: See, earlier I was a bit wrought up with me monthlies, so I'm afraid I didn't watch what I was doing. *(To ELAINE.)* You must have days like this. All we girls do. I suppose, it's one of the things that distinguishes us from the boys. See, I must've closed me eyes while I was washing up, and as a result I accidentally knocked both the mustard and the oil into the water. Then when I looked down, I realised I'd splashed it all over me. But for a moment I thought I'd got infective hepatitis!

ELAINE: 'Infective hepa…'?

JANE: Jaundice, yeah.

HUGHIE: Look, we'd like to be alone!

JANE: Oh, an illicit lunch, is it?

HUGHIE: So if you don't mind, just…

JANE: *(Overriding him.)* Now I remember when I saw you. It was last Sunday afternoon with that redhead, wasn't it?

HUGHIE: Was it?

JANE: Suit yourself.

JANE flounces off behind the bar, singing; 'Hello, young lovers, wherever you are…'.

ELAINE: His dog died, you see.

HUGHIE: Mm?

ELAINE: Trots.

HUGHIE: Trots?

ELAINE: It always did, so he called it 'Trots'.

HUGHIE: And the dog died, and you beat him at Canasta, and then you and he…

ELAINE: Quite.

HUGHIE: Well, must say I'm amazed.

ELAINE: So was he.

HUGHIE: And then Harold came in, did he? While you and his brother were consummating Trot's demise.

ELAINE: No!

HUGHIE: Oh.

ELAINE: I broke it to Harry two days later. Over breakfast.

HUGHIE: Really?

ELAINE: That's when he refused to pay the phone bill, and started to have his boiled egg in the study.

HUGHIE: Listen, I'm getting a bit muddled…

ELAINE: Then you can imagine how *I* feel among the debris! See, there are still toast crumbs and bits of dried egg on his desk. Married for five years, and we always had breakfast together. But after Trots passed on, he even stopped calling me a slut over my Shreddies. And that used to be one of the most poignant moments of our day.

HUGHIE: Bloody hell!

ELAINE: No, I got used to it because Harry's verbal aggression was just a kind of code for him relaying his inner affection for me. Well, he's English in that profoundly sadistic way that gets right through to a woman's heart.

HUGHIE: You poor darling.

ELAINE: But why did it have to happen to me? I only slept with his brother to help Tom over a bad spell. Neither of us really enjoyed it. Well, there was certainly no blaze of glory or anything. He even kept his socks on. A bit like the Duke of Wellington.

HUGHIE: The Duke of...?

ELAINE: Well, he pleasured the Duchess with his Wellington boots on after the Battle of Waterloo, didn't he? Must've been an elated experience for her, knowing she was uppermost in his mind during all that carnage.

Pause.

HUGHIE: So you're...living alone – are you?

ELAINE: *(Seizing his hand.)* Oh, do you want to move in, then? As a...paying guest, or ardent friend?

HUGHIE: *(Gently disengaging his hand.)* No, I'm just trying to understand the ins and outs... I mean, did you er...well, explain to Harry about Trots, Canasta and everything...?

ELAINE pours a large quantity of mayonnaise over her salad, and begins to eat with gusto.

ELAINE: Perhaps if I put on a few pounds, I'll lure him back. He obviously likes the 'big' sort. 'Samantha's built to last,' was the expression I believe he used. But every time *I* overeat, it just goes on my hips. Or even worse, on my knees. *(She swigs back her gin. Then dejectedly she stares at her hands.)* I'm getting older. Actually...older. And by the second. D'you know what I mean?

HUGHIE: No.

ELAINE: Look. *(Pointing at her hand.)* The quality of my skin. It's as if it's been polythene-wrapped.

HUGHIE: You're imagining it. You're just…overwrought.

ELAINE: No, I'm not. Feel!

She holds out her wrist. He strokes it.

HUGHIE: Still got a sexy sheen to it.

ELAINE: *(Shaking her head.)* There's still a superfluity of oil that comes bubbling out of my skin during my sleep.

HUGHIE: My God.

ELAINE: *(Dolefully.)* All my wild strawberries are gone.

HUGHIE: 'Plucked' I thinks the word you're looking for, darling. Yes, it's 'Plucked'.

ELAINE: I should've married you that weekend…

HUGHIE: Yes, but then…well, I've never understood women. Well, not in the way a woman needs to be understood by a man to convince herself she's a woman…if you see what I mean…

In response ELAINE takes hold of HUGHIE's hand, and she rubs his knuckles against her cheek.

ELAINE: Mmmm…you still smell good.

HUGHIE: Thanks. You're pretty aromatic yourself.

ELAINE: *(Nodding.)* Funny the way we just go on chatting, as if there hadn't been nearly a year between.

HUGHIE: Very funny.

ELAINE: If only I had bigger boobs.

HUGHIE: Eh?

ELAINE: Well, Harry's blonde's boobs are outstanding. In every way.

HUGHIE: Oh God!

ELAINE: What's the matter?

HUGHIE points to SIEGFRIED, who is clutching his jacket, which is filled with metal counters, as he stares at ELAINE.

HUGHIE: I think your friend's planning on coming over here.

ELAINE: Then 'Oh God' is right!

HUGHIE: *(Suspicious.)* Why, did you and he…?

ELAINE: No!

HUGHIE: But you do know him, don't you?

ELAINE: Move in with me, Hughie! I promise there'll be no demands. Except the rent, of course.

HUGHIE: *(Indicating SIEGFRIED who is still staring blankly at ELAINE.)* He looks a bit unstable.

ELAINE: Hardly surprising.

HUGHIE: Why?

ELAINE: *(Whispering.)* His house burnt down last week.

HUGHIE: What?!

ELAINE: With his wife in it.

HUGHIE: No!

ELAINE: Yes. And she was in bed at the time.

HUGHIE: Good grief!

ELAINE: Just thought I'd mention it.

HUGHIE: Thanks. So whatever will we talk about?

ELAINE: I should stay off wives and fires, for a start. Oh…and also he's an alcoholic.

HUGHIE: Jumping Jesus!

SIEGFRIED moves over to them, and dumps his coat-full of counters on their table.

SIEGFRIED: *(Full of bonhomie.)* Let me get you good folks a couple of big fat drinks!

HUGHIE: D'you really think you ought to…? I mean, there's no need to.

ELAINE: So how are you, Siggy? *(Realising what she has said.)* Oh God, I'll have another double gin and tonic, with lots of ice, please.

SIEGFRIED: *(Calling out.)* Jane! Another whopping gin and tonic, with a ton of ice, luv.

JANE: Coming up, Siegfried.

SIEGFRIED: *(To HUGHIE.)* Same for you?

HUGHIE: No, brandy! I mean, I'll just have another half of bitter, thank you.

SIEGFRIED: *(To JANE.)* A large brandy, luv, and half a dozen grapefruit juices.

JANE comes over to them.

JANE: Did I hear you right?

SIEGFRIED: No, make it a round dozen grapefruit juices. And in separate glasses. They'll last longer.

SIEGFRIED takes hold of the hem of JANE's pinafore.

JANE: Hey, Siggy, what you up to?

SIEGFRIED pours all the metal counters into the pocket of JANE's pinafore.

SIEGFRIED: And with the change, treat yerself to a large rum and coke.

JANE: Ta very much.

JANE goes over to the bar to prepare the drinks. SIEGFRIED sits next to ELAINE, while HUGHIE finds himself staring at SIEGFRIED's rubicund nose.

SIEGFRIED: Yes, all the veins in me snout have exploded. *(Amused.)* 'Fact under me skin, it must be just like a bullring, after a very gory afternoon.

HUGHIE: Stroll on!

SIEGFRIED picks up a lettuce leaf from ELAINE's plate and munches on it.

SIEGFRIED: It's heartbreaking to win a fortune on oranges, when all I can drink is bleeding grapefruit juice.

ELAINE: Siggy, I was dreadfully sorry to hear about your wife… I mean, oh God!

SIEGFRIED: *(To HUGHIE.)* I'm drying out, see. Up the road. Y'know, in that place they call 'The Castle'.

HUGHIE: You mean, the er…er…

SIEGFRIED: *(Cheerfully.)* Yes, the upmarket nuthouse. Very swish.

HUGHIE: *(At a loss.)* Really?

SIEGFRIED: You should come to tea there sometime. And see the feeding of the menagerie and that. It's highly entertaining.

HUGHIE: Oh, I'm sure it is…

SIEGFRIED: All one's best friends are in there, of course.

HUGHIE: *(Inanely.)* Of course!

SIEGFRIED: And if they're not in there, it's only because they can't afford it.

HUGHIE: But you…can.

SIEGFRIED: No.

HUGHIE: Oh.

SIEGFRIED: I had to borrow the fees from me aunt. She'll never get it back, though, but then she comes from St. Helens soshe is philosophical.

HUGHIE: And you're in the Castle because you're a…a…

SIEGFRIED: *(Enjoying himself.)* An alcoholic, yes! Well, that's what you told him I was, isn't it, Elaine?

ELAINE: Well, I may have dropped the odd hint…

SIEGFRIED: *(To HUGHIE.)* She's right on the button. 'Cause I'm the local piss artist! Well, it comes easy if you're born that way. You might almost say it's a terrific, malefic gift. Certainly gives me focus.

ELAINE: God, I could do with a drink!.. *(Quickly.)* …of tea or something.

JANE comes over with a large tray of drinks.

JANE: Here you are, luv.

Grinning SIEGFRIED counts the twelve glasses of grapefruit juice while ELAINE and HUGHIE look on in amazement.)

SIEGFRIED: Cheers!

ELAINE: Skol!

HUGHIE: Prost!

SIEGFRIED swigs back three glasses one after another.

SIEGRFRIED: It's important to keep me throat-muscles in trim, you see - in case I can't hold out.

HUGHIE: Yes, why *have* they let you out? *(Correcting himself.)* Sorry, I didn't mean…

SIEGFRIED: 'Cause they don't count alcoholism as insanity. At least not in the national averages.

(HUGHIE swigs back his brandy.)

JANE: *(To HUGHIE.)* I just don't understand why you men have this thing about redheads.

HUGHIE: Some men don't. 'Fact her hubby has a penchant for fecund blondes with outstanding boobs.

ELAINE: Oh, it's always so delightful discussing one's most intimate secrets with you, Hughie.

SIEGFRIED swigs back another grapefruit juice.

SIEGFRIED: There's a man – in the bin – who's been there since it opened. Says the food's steadily gone downhill. Ever since the butcher was certified. Funny what happens to a man when you take his chopper off him.

ELAINE: How's *your* year been, Hughie?

HUGHIE: Well, actually it's been…

JANE: *(Overriding him.) I* got pregnant this spring.

HUGHIE: Huh?

JANE: Happens nearly every April. Always look on it as a kind of rest from me monthlies. But never amounts to much, though.

SIEGFRIED: *(After swigging his fifth grapefruit.)* Most things don't.

JANE: There's a lot of wind involved.

SIEGFRIED: Generally is.

(SIEGFRIED burps.)

JANE: My doctor says it's just Nature extending my superb potential to its full. He's one of them jokey quacks, y'know. When he examines me, he pants a lot and makes what he thinks are cute quips. Like – 'It's always a pleasure to tinker with a well-kept chassis, Miss Parsons.' Or – 'I'm sure this is doing more for me than it is for you.' *(To ELAINE.)* Men are so juvenile, don't you find? *(To the MEN.)* Present company excepted, of course.

HUGHIE: How many er…children have you…er got, then?

JANE: 'Bout four. 'Least that was the last count. Though their fathers are prone to exaggerate.

ELAINE: Fathers?!

SIEGFRIED: Yes, Jane, exactly how many male progenitors are there?

SIEGFRIED swigs back his sixth fruit juice.

ELAINE: Oh…two or three. I've never been one for numerical complacency.

HUGHIE: I beg your pardon?

ELAINE: Oh didn't you know? I'm not only a Reader's Digest expert, but I'm very hands-on with Roget's.

HUGHIE: Who?

ELAINE: Thesaurus, luv.

HUGHIE: Oh.

JANE: Now there's no need to look at me like that. Just 'cause a few of me vowels are off, it doesn't mean I'm semantically deficient.

ELAINE: Admit it, Jane. You're really pulling our legs about you having all those children, aren't you?

JANE: No. Though it's the actual child-bearing that I find unproductive. I mean, who wants to be a nine-month receptacle for some little bastard, who's bound to make your life hell as soon as it can toddle?

ELAINE: I say, that's a bit strong.

JANE: Well, the little sods always do, don't they? Just to prove they're related to you.

SIEGFRIED: There's this girl in the bin, who keeps following me about. She's probably waiting for me outside now. And she keeps shouting at me; 'Rover! Rover!'

HUGHIE: And how do you…respond?

SIEGFRIED: I bark, of course. I'm not a complete fool.

JANE: So why doesn't the girl come in?

SIEGFRIED: She just won't.

JANE: But why?

SIEGFRIED: She doesn't think I'm supposed to be here in the first place, and so, in a way – to *her* – I'm not.

JANE: I still don't under…

SIEGFRIED: *(Overriding her.)* Haven't you read your sign out there on the pub door?

JANE: What sign?

SIEGFRIED: NO DOGS ALLOWED! *(Everyone but SIEGFRIED laughs.)* Ay, that's what it's all about, isn't it?

HUGHIE: Huh?

SIEGFRIED: The joke. It's like the captions on my cartoons.

HUGHIE: I don't follow…

SIEGFRIED: Laughter always comes out of someone else's pain.

(He swigs back his seventh fruit juice.)

JANE: Yes, well…would er…everyone like some coffee?

SIEGFRIED: Being a shade too semantical, am I?

ELAINE: *(To JANE.)* I'd love a coffee, thank you.

HUGHIE: Me, too, please.

JANE: My latest lover says that seriousness is a thing of the remote past. And according to him, it's all because of the British Empire.

HUGHIE: Bit of an obtuse observation, isn't it?

JANE: Well, Billy always says; 'In days of yore, when we had the Empire, we hadn't got time to laugh because we were too busy making all the natives cry. But now we're free of the Empire, and perpetually broke into the bargain, we giggle inanely from morning 'till night'.

SIEGFRIED: Oh what a clear thinker your Billy is in this age of anarchic mediocrity.

SIEGFRIED swigs back his eighth fruit juice.

JANE: That's what I like about my Billy. He's so succinct in his summaries of world history. Mind, I never question any of his endless generalisations, 'cause that would play havoc with his image of himself. *(To ELAINE.)* Well, men pride themselves on their innate ability to think logically, don't they? That's why it's always dangerous for us to challenge them with anything relating specifically to the human condition. See, men are just post-pubescent, Priapic Peter Pans. The last thing a man likes to deal with is any form of reality. And if you argue with them – especially if you're right and they're wrong, which is generally the case – it makes them very violently excitable. And as a result, I usually end up on my back in bed! 'Cause sex seems to be their solution to everything. Even to the over-population crisis. *(To the MEN.)* You're such reasonable creatures in debate amongst yourselves, and yet you're all so frenzied when it comes to impotence. Milk and sugar for everyone?

Pause.

HUGHIE: Which University did you go to?

JANE: I didn't.

HUGHIE: Oh come on....

JANE: I'm self-taught. In every way. *(To EVERYONE.)* So which do you want, or do you want neither?

HUGHIE: Er…both, with two sugars, please.

ELAINE: *(Acidly.)* Neither of either, thanks.

JANE: Funny, the way you two think that intelligence is just the prerogative of the Southern Counties. And very pathetic.

JANE goes behind the bar to make the coffee.

SIEGFRIED: *(Grinning at ELAINE.)* Gone off the Irish coffee and whipped cream, have we?

ELAINE: What?!

SIEGFRIED: *(To HUGHIE.)* First time I took her out, she absolutely floored me with her inordinately-expensive tastes.

SIEGFRIED swigs back his ninth fruit juice.

HUGHIE: *(To ELAINE.)* But I thought you said that you and Siggy had never…?

ELAINE: *(Quickly.)* I think I should explain, Hughie darling. You see…

SIEGFRIED: *(Overriding her.)* Cost me a proverbial fortune.

ELAINE: Now, now, Siggy!

SIEGFRIED: What's more, at the time I was employed by her skinflint of a husband.

ELAINE: *(With relief.)* Oh, you meant on *that* occasion.

SIEGFRIED: *(Mischievously.)* Oh, did you think I meant the *other* occasions?

ELAINE: Well, I wasn't absolutely certain.

SIEGFRIED: *(To HUGHIE.)* So on *this* occasion, I said to her, 'What would you like for starters. Grapefruit segments, home-made rough patè, avocado or gefilter fish?' And y'know what she said?

HUGHIE: No.

SIEGFRIED: 'I'll just have half a lobster, please, with a brace of grouse to follow.'

HUGHIE: *(To ELAINE.)* You didn't?!

SIEGFRIED: She did. And she rounded it off with Bombe Surprise, goat's cheese and Irish coffee with double cream.

HUGHIE: Holy cow!

SIEGFRIED: And when I squeezed her knee under the table while she was lapping her way through the double cream to get to the booze, d'you know what she said?

HUGHIE: I daren't guess.

SIEGFRIED: She said, 'Please, Siegfried, don't let's spoil a beautiful lunch with the ugly preliminaries of lust.'

HUGHIE: Stroll on.

ELAINE: Well, I was only just married, so I thought I'd show a little will power.

SIEGFRIED: You could've fooled me and my bank manager. *(Suddenly aggressive.)* As for your bloody husband…!

ELAINE: There's no need to bring him into it.

SIEGFRIED: D'you realise I've not worked for the best part of three years, Elaine! And that's including for your bastard husband and his sodding magazine. Yet I'm one of the best cartoonists there is. But who employs me? The Loony Bin! Where there's always a nurse, tapping me on the shoulder, and asking me which cheek of my arse I'd like the needle in. Can't sleep, see, so they use a syringe the size of a Christmas cracker, and then they squirt me full of dreams.

He pretends to inject ELAINE with a fork, who jumps out of her seat.

ELAINE: Please, Siggy, stop. I can't bear it!

SIEGFRIED: Mind, I'm surprised your Harry hasn't won the Nobel Prize for groping.

ELAINE: *(Sitting down again.)* Oh shut up, Siggy, shut up!

SIEGFRIED: 'Fact his secretary's the only girl I've seen doing two hundred words a minute, while she's running round her desk at the same time.

ELAINE: I said shut up! SHUT UP!

SIEGFRIED: With her pad in one hand, and her knickers in the other.

ELAINE: It's not true. Harry's not like that. Well, only with fecund, busty blondes. Oh God!

Sobbing she leaps to her feet again and moves away from the table. HUGHIE half follows her.

HUGHIE: Where you going, darling?

ELAINE: Leave me alone. Just leave me alone!

She bangs her way into 'The Ladies' on the opposite side of the Lounge.

HUGHIE: *(Sitting.)* There was no need for that.

SIEGFRIED: That's what I meant.

HUGHIE: *(Preoccupied.)* Mm?

SIEGFRIED: About humour. You cut succulent slices off someone, and *other* people laugh. Then your scalpel slips, and you're into the bone. And all you're left with is a bloodbath. But then, of course, comedy is tragedy speeded up. *(He swigs back his eleventh fruit juice.)* Were you lovers long?

HUGHIE: I don't see what that's got to do with you!

SIEGFRIED: *We* weren't. Just a couple of weeks.

HUGHIE: I think you've said more than enough.

SIEGFRIED: Did you notice she's got a funny way of kissing? Closes her eyes and opens her mouth. *(Demonstrating.)*Very disconcerting.

HUGHIE: Look, you've got no right to…

SIEGFRIED: *(Overriding him.)* But it couldn't go on. Crayfish out of season and champagne for elevenses. 'Fact my bank-manager took me to one side and asked me if I was trying to emulate the National Debt.

He swigs back his last fruit juice.

HUGHIE: Jesus, you've drunk all twelve!

SIEGFRIED: I was walking along this road yesterday afternoon, when this girl – y'know, the one who keeps following me about – well, suddenly she shouts at me; 'Heel, Rover, heel!'

HUGHIE: Look, Siggy, I'm not interested in…

SIEGFRIED: *(Overriding him.)* And there was this snooty-looking lady who was just about to pass me, but instead Mrs Snooty stopped directly in front of me. Then she peered down at her miniature poodle - who obviously wasn't called 'Rover' - and then she looked up at me. I suppose because I had my tongue out at the time, and I was panting. Then she gave her overgrown rat a tug just as it was about to pee on my shoes and said, 'Naughty, naughty, Esmerelda! I'll find you a nice lamp-post 'cause I can't have you flirting with cross-bred mongrels.'

HUGHIE: So what did you do? Growl and run back to your nutty mistress?

(Pause.)

SIEGFRIED: Insanity's a strange thing, lad. It's often brought on by an apparently-harmless fetish. By some mental aberration that's been stretched beyond its natural limits.

Though who knows what's 'natural' for anyone else. I don't know what's natural for you, or you for me. But suddenly this fetish builds into a mind-tearing obsession. And we've all got one, tapping away inside us, and much nearer to exploding than we think. 'Fact every cartoon I've ever drawn has tinkered with the trappings of madness, and often without me even being aware of it. So constantly we all make lots of jokes to show we don't care how precariously-insignificant we are. *(While he talks, almost unconsciously he uses his empty glasses to build a precarious structure.)* You see, we know only too well that if we don't laugh at ourselves, this terrible desire for permanence that we have deep inside us, it will eat right through our sanity - until we're raw like oysters. And that's how they are in the loony bin. Just bloody raw oysters. And any fetish can set it off, y'know. The way you keep brushing that invisible dandruff off your left shoulder, for instance. *(HUGHIE rubs his hands together self-consciously.)* Oh didn't you realise you do that? *(Without thinking HUGHIE straightens his cutlery.)* And your perpetual re-arranging of your cutlery.

HUGHIE: Look, I don't have to sit here listening to you…!

SIEGFRIED: Indeed you don't, but my wife used to place her hairbrush on her dressing table exactly a thumb's breadth away from her lipstick. So it can be the most innocuous ritual. Any bizarre relationship with an inanimate object will do. Then one morning the hairbrush became too much for my wife. Its lack of coherence began to gnaw at her. Then it started to haunt her. And on that fateful morning, finally it possessed her. And then she – with such a profound sense of relief – gave into her hairbrush.

HUGHIE: Oh please don't go on about your poor wife!

SIEGFRIED: Then there's this woman in the asylum who cleans the same windows hour after hour, until they're too bright to even reflect her own image. And on a fine day, when the sun hits them, the windows blaze like polished gongs. You can almost *hear* the light being thrown back off the glass, in a sort of continuous applause for the miracle of sunshine. But this woman doesn't notice that. She just keeps relentlessly rubbing and polishing the windows, trying to take the very skin off her knuckles, and off the glass. *(Breaking down.)* It's as if she wants to be cleaner than the sunshine itself. Oh God, dear God… *(HUGHIE touches his shoulder reassuringly.)* Sorry…just came over me. Anything can do it. Doesn't have to be related…

JANE comes over with their coffee.

JANE: You alright, Siggy?

SIEGFRIED: *(Going into his gag routine.)* Abso-bloody-lutely! Was just telling our friend about this man who still collects 1950s condoms. He saves 'em up like stamps. So now he's got over a hundred boxes of rubber bliss, all decomposing in a suitcase. *(He sips his coffee as ELAINE appears, looking distraught.)* And he told me he was getting married to an Alderman – or was it an Alderwoman? Well, it was certainly to somebody in the Town Hall. Nice coffee.

ELAINE: *(To HUGHIE.)* I'd like to go now, please.

SIEGFRIED: *(To ELAINE.)* So you've noticed, have you?

ELAINE: Pardon?

SIEGFRIED: I talk like I used to drink; too much and too often.

ELAINE: No, that's not the reason I want to…

SIEGFRIED: *(Overriding her.)* You're a nice woman. You always look so delectably clean and pampered.

JANE: And I suppose *I* don't?

SIEGFRIED: *(Grinning.)* No, you look used and appreciated. Which is even nicer.

ELAINE: Charming!

SIEGFRIED: One minute I was walking along my road, and the next minute I was running. It was as if my legs had got a will of their own…

ELAINE: *(Frightened.)* Take me home, Hughie. Please!

HUGHIE: Sure…

SIEGFRIED: Then I smelt it. Suddenly I knew *why* my legs were running 'cause there was all this smoke rasping the back of my throat. Then I saw my whole cottage going up in a welter of flames. And I stopped in my tracks. Just stopped! And I thought; 'Well, that's that, then.' *(Grinning.)* I'm so conditioned, I even envisaged the headlines; 'CARTOONIST'S COTTAGE GOES UP IN A PUFF OF JOKES!' *(JANE touches his arm.)* 'S'alright, luv, I'm done. I'll be cured soon, and I'll start working again – filling in all those balloons. Then I might find out why everything's so bloody funny. *(To ELAINE.)* Well, give your bastard husband my regards. 'Cause you're lucky, lass, damned lucky.

Impulsively he hugs her.

ELAINE: Lucky's the last thing I am!

SIEGFRIED wanders back to the fruit machine.

HUGHIE: She's right, Siggy! See, Harry's gone off with a busty, blonde, fecund floozy! *(Realising what he's said.)* Oh God, let's get the hell outta here.

As HUGHIE rises to go out with ELAINE, absently SIEGFRIED taps the fruit machine, which instantly disgorges more metal counters.)

SIEGFRIED: Oh no!

HUGHIE: Incredible.

SIEGFRIED: I didn't even put a thing in it. Jane, do me a favour, luv, will you? Tell that girl out there, that's waiting for me, to bring my sodding lead in before I empty this godforsaken machine.

ELAINE pulls HUGHIE over to the bar.

ELAINE: I need a drink!

HUGHIE: But you've already had…

ELAINE: *(Overriding him.)* We came here to talk about *us*, and all we did was talk about *him*!

SIEGFRIED wins on the fruit machine again and roars with rage.

JANE: *(To HUGHIE.)* But I thought you…

HUGHIE: So did I!

ELAINE waves at JANE, who is behind the bar.

ELAINE: Triple brandies all round, please.

JANE: Fuck a duck.

ELAINE: If that's your taste. *(To JANE.)* But get us the brandies quick, love.

HUGHIE: I didn't know that you and Siegfried had been… well, intimate?

ELAINE: It only lasted a fortnight.

HUGHIE: Really?

ELAINE: See, Harold wanted Siggy's cartoons delivered on time.

HUGHIE: So you bent over his desk to give him inspiration.

ELAINE: No, we only had rumpy-pumpy after a very expensive lunch. It was the only way I could think to try and keep Siggy sober, so he could deliver on time.

HUGHIE: And did it work?

ELAINE: No, he used to drink himself senseless after our rumpy-pumpy to recover from the shock of paying the restaurant bill.

JANE comes over with the drinks as SIEGFRIED wins again on the fruit machine.

JANE: Here you are, folks.

HUGHIE: He's not still winning, is he?

He hands JANE some money.

JANE: 'Course. But I'll keep all the change 'cause I've earned it.

She goes off.

ELAINE: According to the Coroner, Siegfried's wife accidentally set herself alight while she was pouring herself a scotch because she had a smouldering cigarette in one hand and a lighted match in the other.

HUGHIE: Oh she wasn't a boozer, too, was she?

ELAINE: You bet ya. She and Siggy kind of competed. Each had their own waste bin. And at the end of every week, the one with the most empties won an engraved corkscrew, and also was allowed to tear another photograph out of their wedding album.

HUGHIE: Bleeding hell! *(In desperation.)* How's your mother?

ELAINE: Dead!

HUGHIE: Oh no!

ELAINE: Oh yes. See, Mum tripped while she was switching the telly off.

HUGHIE: But surely switching the telly off…?

ELAINE: *(Overriding him.)* Mum used to keep the telly in an alcove at the top the stairs.

HUGHIE: She didn't.

ELAINE: She did. See, she didn't want to become addicted to it, so she used to watch it while moving from the bedroom to the bathroom. Kind of en passant.

HUGHIE: Siegfried's abso-bloody-lutely right.

ELAINE: What?

HUGHIE: We're all just fucking raw oysters!

ELAINE: No, it was News Night that did it. She tried to turn off the Chancellor of the Exchequer, and she tripped over her nightie…

HUGHIE: And she fell down stairs…

ELAINE: Yes, and in the process she broke both arms, her left hip and her neck.

HUGHIE: And Bob's your uncle.

ELAINE: *(Wailing.)* Don't mock the dead! *(Wiping her tears.)* So now you'd better tell me about your year.

HUGHIE: I don't think it would interest you.

ELAINE: You're probably right. But you will come to her funeral on Friday, won't you? They've had to keep her in the fridge over the Bank Holiday. I hope nothing's sagged or anything.

HUGHIE: Sorry, but… I can't.

ELAINE: Why?

HUGHIE: I'm getting married on Friday.

ELAINE: *(Howling.)* Oh, how lovely for you!

HUGHIE: Isn't it?

ELAINE: And she must be the redhead that the barmaid saw you with last Sunday, right?

HUGHIE: Right. And after the wedding this Saturday, Jennifer and I are going on safari for our honeymoon in South Africa.

ELAINE: Not only has my mother dropped dead, my husband walked out on me, and you're marrying and rogering a redhead, but to cap it all, this morning Tyger followed suit.

HUGHIE: Tyger?

ELAINE: Our promiscuous cat. Like my husband, Tyger did a bunk on me, too, and the little slut's left me with fourteen kittens. Talking of which, you wouldn't care for the odd dozen kitties, would you?

HUGHIE: No, Jennifer's allergic to fur.

ELAINE: So am I! *(She rushes to the door wailing. HUGHIE is about to follow her.)* No, no, Hughie, stay there! It's been lovely seeing you. And I just can't wait to reminisce with you this time next year. But, for Christ's sake, don't come here unless you're getting divorced, you've caught leprosy, and your mother's snuffed it!

She rushes out of the pub, and simultaneously the fruit machine starts making terrible noises.

SIEGFRIED: *(Jubilant.)* Thank God for that!

JANE reappears.

JANE: Now what's up, luv?

SIEGFRIED: The machine's busted.

JANE: Not surprising.

SIEGFRIED: 'Fact it's started vomiting nuts and bolts in protest.

Triumphantly he holds up various bits of the fruit machine.

Blackout.

The End

AN EVENING WITH THE G.L.C.
A PLAY IN ONE ACT

Characters

COUNCILLOR RENNIP

CLIFF

TOM

FLOOR MANAGER

An Evening With The G.L.C. was first performed at the Soho Poly, London on 12th February 1974 with the following cast;

COUNCILLOR RENNIP, Michael Godfrey

CLIFF, Timothy Munro

TOM, Graham Lines

FLOOR MANAGER, Tom Durham

Director, Walter Hall

Designer, Rudy Stussi

A television news studio. 1974.

COUNCILLOR RENNIP and his son, CLIFF, are sitting opposite the TV interviewer, TOM BOLTON.

Behind them we see the name of the programme 'CONFRONTATION', while the FLOOR MANAGER, with his earphones on, is buzzing around them.

FLOOR MANAGER: Everyone happy? You comfortable, Councillor?

COUNCILLOR: Yes, but I'd hardly say I was happy.

FLOOR MANAGER: Well, there's two minutes to go.

TOM: You *are* going to go through with it, though, Councillor Rennip, aren't you?

COUNCILLOR: I don't know, Tom. It's risky.

TOM: Cliff?

CLIFF: Part of me agrees with Dad, Mr Bolton…

TOM: Oh *you're* not going to back down on me as well, are you, Cliff?

CLIFF: Well, if Dad thinks it's dicey, I don't feel we should go against…

FLOOR MANAGER: *(Listening through his earphones.)* What? Oh! *(To CLIFF.)* Cliff, don't touch the mike. It's pretty ear-shattering up there.

CLIFF: Oh sorry, I didn't mean to.

TOM: No, seriously, Councillor. It's bound to do your political image a power of good. And it'll make great television.

COUNCILLOR: *(Dryly.)* Yeah, I'm sure it will.

TOM: Then why are you so hesitant?

COUNCILLOR: Oh I'm not saying the Labour Party couldn't do with a new face-lift, but I still say it's bordering on the unethical. I mean, what kind of questions are you going to throw at me?

FLOOR MANAGER: *(Pointing to the monitor above their heads.)* Studio, settle down, please. We'll be on as soon as the News is finished.

CLIFF: When's that?

FLOOR MANAGER: One minute from now.

COUNCILLOR: Look, Tom, I definitely think we should stick to our original...

TOM: Oh come on, Councillor, let's reveal the truth for once. It's a unique opportunity.

COUNCILLOR: But it could easily misfire.

TOM: It won't. And it'll show the public that all politicians are not the hypocritical crooks you're made out to be.

COUNCILLOR: Thanks very much for nothing.

TOM: I didn't mean to be derogatory. *(Watching the COUNCILLOR swallowing a pill with water.)* Have you got indigestion or something?

COUNCILLOR: *(Shaking his head.)* Just a half-hearted ulcer.

FLOOR MANAGER: Quiet, everyone, please! Thirty seconds.

CLIFF: *(To the COUNCILLOR.)* Mr Bolton's got a point, Dad. It'll show you're not scared of being interviewed in depth, and that you do speak the truth.

COUNCILLOR: I don't know, Cliff. You've got some strange ideas...

TOM: *(Interrupting.)* Look on it, Councillor, as a P.R. job for the Labour Party, and for you in particular.

FLOOR MANAGER: Would everyone please be quiet!?

COUNCILLOR: I still say...

FLOOR MANAGER: Please, Councillor. Fifteen seconds.

TOM: *(Under his breath to his Guests.)* Best of luck, Councillor. And you, too, Cliff.

FLOOR MANAGER: Stand by. Stand by!

COUNCILLOR: But we haven't agreed…

FLOOR MANAGER: *(Overriding him.)* PLEASE! 10 seconds…87654….

The FLOOR MANAGER cues TOM.

TOM: Good evening. As this is the last of the present series of 'Confrontation', I thought it would be refreshing if the programme tonight had a twist to it. Instead of me interviewing Mr Vic Rennip, the prominent Labour Councillor for East Stratton, Cliff Rennip is going to interview his father instead. So this is not a political interview as such, because it is a son questioning his father about the problems that the Councillor has to face combining his family life, with his obligations to the community at large. But once again it proves that the Councillor is one of the few politicians, who regards the truth as being more important than political expediency. Also before we start, I would like to assure you that no one in this studio, myself included, has had any prior knowledge as to the form, or nature, of Cliff's questions. So there should be a big surprise all round.

COUNCILLOR: *(Smiling.)* You can say that again.

TOM: *(Standing.)* Now I have the pleasure of vacating the Chair in favour of Cliff Rennip. Cliff?

CLIFF: *(Crossing to TOM's seat and sitting down.)* Oh thank you, Mr Bolton. *(Pause.)* Well er…here goes. *(Pause.)* Can I er… ask anything?

TOM: It's *your* show.

CLIFF: You mean, it doesn't matter…what kind of question I ask?

COUNCILLOR: No. As long as it's within reason.

CLIFF: *(Grinning.)* It's difficult to know *what's* 'within reason', though, isn't it, Dad?

COUNCILLOR: Oh you're not going to start indulging in semantics immediately, are you?

CLIFF: I just want to define the boundaries. So we can get at the truth.

COUNCILLOR: *(Good humoured.)* Look, I'm sure you've a very clear idea of the questions that would interest our viewers. You're quite an expert on communication. They didn't make you Deputy Head Prefect for nothing now, did they?

CLIFF: I'm trying to avoid…well, offending you, Dad, that's all.

COUNCILLOR: Hm! It's pretty obvious you've a blockbuster of a question you're dying to drop on me. So, for goodness sake, drop it. *(Pause.)* Well, go on.

CLIFF: It's…well, it's rather…embarrassing.

COUNCILLOR: *(Smiling.)* It'll be even more embarrassing if everyone switches off. So fire away.

CLIFF: Well, it's about Mum actually…

COUNCILLOR: Whatever's your mother got to do with the Council?

CLIFF: Well, I sometimes wonder if…well, because of your career and that…and, because of your obligations to the Council and society in general that…well, I just wonder if Mum suffers?

COUNCILLOR: Suffers?

CLIFF: What I mean is…well, do *you* think she suffers?

COUNCILLOR: In what way?

CLIFF: Well, she doesn't see that much of you, does she? With all the hours you have to work and that…and I mean, well, Mum is always stuck at home and…

COUNCILLOR: *(Smiling.)* Only because she prefers it that way. You know perfectly well that public appearances and election campaigning make her nervous and shy. And it's perfectly understandable because she happens to enjoy the quiet life. So it's nothing to do with her suffering at all. *(To TOM.)* As I am sure she explained to you, when she declined to appear on *your* show tonight, Tom. *(Chuckling.)* She prefers watching *me* making funny faces instead. *(To CLIFF.)* And, anyway, Cliff, I don't think this is a very profitable line of questioning. I think it would interest the viewers more if we…say, discussed the difficulties of being a politician's son?

CLIFF: You mean, you want us to talk about the way politics stop you and me communicating, Dad?

COUNCILLOR: Well, no, I didn't mean that exactly. I mean more the way that you have to put up with your friends saying derogatory things about me…and, well, politics in general.

CLIFF: True, they do.

COUNCILLOR: Must be very hurtful.

CLIFF: Can be.

COUNCILLOR: And it must be a terrible strain on you, always being forced to…well, defend my politics and…

CLIFF: *(Overriding him.)* I don't.

(Pause.)

COUNCILLOR: *(Trying to laugh it off.)* Oh, really?

CLIFF: No. I'm afraid I can't defend you.

TOM: *(Leaning forward.)* Why not?

CLIFF: I'd like to but…

TOM: But what?

COUNCILLOR: Stop prompting him, Tom. He's quite capable of speaking his mind, I assure you. Anyway, there's no reason he should support my political beliefs. Our family is not a totalitarian state. He has the complete freedom to believe exactly what he wants.

CLIFF: Now don't get me wrong, Dad. I'd stand up for you any day – as my father – and against absolutely anyone. It's just, well…I have problems with you as a politician. *(Turning to TOM.)* Mr Bolton, you'd better ask the questions. I'm no good at this…

TOM: You can't get out of it as easily as that, Cliff. We want to see your father as both a politician and as a complete man. So let's have your next question, please?

CLIFF: Do I have to?

COUNCILLOR: Yes, son. This is the opportunity you've been waiting for. You're always saying; 'I'd like to have a go at you in public, Dad.' Well, we couldn't be more public now if we tried. So come on; have a go, Joe.

CLIFF: OK, but before I do, I want you to know that I think you're a damn good father. Despite everything. Look, I'm sorry if it's embarrassing you, but I just want you to know that.

COUNCILLOR: Well, thanks, Cliff. It's mutual. *(Laughing, to TOM.)* So what exactly is it you want to ask me?

CLIFF: Well, Dad, it's about what's true…and what's not true.

COUNCILLOR: *(Mystified.)* Sorry?

CLIFF: See, I don't understand how you can be so…well, straightforward at home. I mean in your personal relationships with me and Mum, and yet in public you're so…well…

COUNCILLOR: *(Overriding him.)* I'm afraid you've lost me, Cliff. How about you, Tom?

TOM: Oh no, I'm fascinated. As I'm sure the viewers are. So do go on, Cliff. Please.

CLIFF: What I'm getting at, Dad, is this. Why do you make politics so unnecessarily…tortuous, and so difficult? I mean, why do you say one thing to Mum and me about a particular policy, and then you go to a Council meeting and say something entirely different? Just doesn't make sense.

COUNCILLOR: *(After taking another pill.)* You're the one who's not making any sense, Cliff!

CLIFF: Alright, Dad, I'll be specific.

COUNCILLOR: That'll be a breakthrough.

CLIFF: D'you mind if I ask you some specific questions about the Council?

COUNCILLOR: *(Disconcerted.)* Specific questions about the…?

CLIFF: *(Overriding him.)* Yeah. D'you mind?

COUNCILLOR*: (Trying to hide his concern.)* No, no, of course not. *(Grinning.)* But we don't want to turn this into a Party Political Broadcast, do we? Or Ted Heath'll go all petulant on us. And we know what that leads to; all the Council's assets'll get frozen.

The COUNCILLOR laughs heartily.

CLIFF: I'm just trying to get at the truth, Dad, that's all.

COUNCILLOR: The er…'truth' as you call it, is a pretty big word.

CLIFF: Yes, isn't it?

COUNCILLOR: Would you recognise the truth if you saw it?

CLIFF: I think so. Yeah, I would. Absolutely.

COUNCILLOR: Wish I had your confidence.

CLIFF: You taking the Mickey, Dad?

COUNCILLOR: No. it's just I've generally found the…so-called truth to be a two-headed axe. Especially if it's used indiscriminately. Which is generally the case. And then you can end up with blood all over you. Other people's blood.

CLIFF: You're not suggesting in that rather colourful language of yours, Dad, that certain facts about the G.L.C. are better hidden from general public view, are you?

COUNCILLOR: I'm not suggesting anything.

CLIFF: You're hedging again.

COUNCILLOR: It all depends on what the facts are, doesn't it? And also on what you're going to do with the truth when you get it. The truth can be often cruel and vicious, and sometimes totally destructive. Is it wise to open Pandora's box, and let out Stalin?

CLIFF: Oh cut the rhetorical polemic, Dad! Let's get back to specifics. I'm going to read you something you said the other day.

COUNCILLOR: What do you mean you're 'going to read me something I said'…

CLIFF: *(Overriding him and waving a notebook in his face.)* Well, as we're getting down to the nitty-gritty, you might as well know that this programme has been set-up for over a fortnight.

COUNCILLOR: What?!

CLIFF: Yeah, Mr Bolton rang me up and asked me if I would be interested in…

COUNCILLOR: *(Interrupting.)* Is this true, Tom?

TOM: Well, yes, I did say to Cliff that I felt that you were one of the very politicians who could er…stand up to his son's scrutiny.

COUNCILLOR: Oh that's what you call it, is it?

TOM: But I assure you, Councillor, I never suggested Cliff should make notes or anything.

CLIFF: No, that was *my* idea, Dad. And, of course, Mum agreed.

COUNCILLOR: Your mother's not in this plot as well, is she?

CLIFF: You bet ya. You see, she thought it would be best if I wrote down everything you said that was politically relevant in this notebook. I mean, we all know how much you hate being misquoted. It makes you go all paranoid, doesn't it?

COUNCILLOR: *(Trying to laugh it off.)* What utter nonsense. Though I can't understand why she didn't tell me. Your Mum's never been able to keep a secret in her life.

CLIFF: *(Consulting his notes.)* You said over breakfast last Thursday at 8.27 precisely… and I must say I found it difficult to work out what you really meant…

COUNCILLOR: Look, dispense with the preamble, and let's just have the bombshell.

CLIFF: You said – and I quote… *(Reading.)* 'There's always a great gap between what I *believe* in as a private individual, and what I have to *do* as a politician for the sake of the Labour Party.' Then you cast your eyes to Heaven and added… *(Reading.)* 'I've got to be careful not to rock the boat as we're nearly on the rocks as it is.'

COUNCILLOR: *(Laughing.)* And I thought you were just making notes on Biology.

CLIFF: In a way, I *was*.

COUNCILLOR: *(Still laughing.)* Did I really say that?

CLIFF: And more.

COUNCILLOR: Extraordinary.

CLIFF: Isn't it?

COUNCILLOR: Oh stop being so pompous, Cliff. You know perfectly well any quotation in politics taken out of context…well, it can give a totally misleading impression.

CLIFF: You also said… *(Reading.)* 'It's sad, Martha, but often I'm forced into having to ignore the promptings of my social conscience in order not to upset our non-existent Party unity'. I remember you emphasising 'non-existent'.

COUNCILLOR: Well, you remember a sight more than I do.

CLIFF: Yeah, but what I don't understand is how a man of your…well, avowed principles can be so…well, hypocritical.

COUNCILLOR: Look, son, why don't we discuss something on which we're both experts? Like…well, like cricket, for instance.

CLIFF: I thought this was supposed to be a serious programme.

COUNCILLOR: Cricket *is* serious!

TOM: Oh come now, Councillor, I think Cliff's question about personal morality being sacrificed to political expediency is a very important question.

COUNCILLOR: It is, indeed. But it's also a very complex and paradoxical question. And emotive words like 'personal morality' and 'political expedience' give the whole subject a contorted bias which can cloud the issue.

CLIFF: Now who's playing at semantics?

COUNCILLOR: You must realise there are no simple answers to the political problems that are facing Britain at this moment. Every move we make is inter-related. Not to mention chain-reactive. So concepts like 'universal good' and 'the real truth' are purely philosophical ideals, and they have little to do with being a day-to-day politician. Especially in a country like ours, which is over-populated, underpaid, over-taxed, and pathetically short on natural resources. Yes, and don't be misled by the oil-finds in the North Sea. At the rate we're going with our inflation, we'll have sold off our oil birthright to the U.S. and the Common Market, long before the oil reaches the pipelines, simply to survive and rectify our Balance of Payments' deficit in the interim. The point I'm getting at is this. We are the clapped-out remains of the greatest Empire the world has ever known. Yet we haven't got used to the idea that we have to work for our living. Especially as there isn't a lot of work around. But we do have to work, or sink. For the first time for two centuries, Not-So-'Great'-Britain has to fend for itself. So we're having to re-assess our thinking about ourselves, and our Democracy. But most painful of all, we're having to come to terms with our impotence on the world stage. And at the moment, the end product is chaos. Especially economically. I mean, it's only too obvious that Unions and Management are ill-prepared for the open competition in world markets. And socially we're uncoordinated, and still poisoned with class prejudice and comparative poverty. In fact, as a nation, we're split right down the middle. So whatever reforms we enact, and whatever incentives we offer to industry, the result is the same. The reforms alienate one half of the population, while the incentives alienate the other half. It's just ring-a-ring-a-roses, and 'Atishoo, atishoo, we all fall down!' So for every step we take forward, generally we take at least three backwards! So who is right? Who is moral? And who is hypocritical?

CLIFF: Have you finished, Dad?

COUNCILLOR: For the moment.

CLIFF: Good. Now perhaps you'll answer the question I asked you.

COUNCILLOR: I just have.

CLIFF: Oh get real, Dad!

COUNCILLOR: That's exactly what I've done. I've put it into a 'realistic' political context.

CLIFF: Yes, Dad, but all that guff you've just spouted has got nothing to do with why you *believe* one thing, and *do* another!

COUNCILLOR: It has everything to do with it. Now look, Cliff, you know that I have certain pet reforms of my own that I would like to implement in my borough. But for the time being I have had to thrust them into the background. And why? Because I feel it's my duty to put my full weight and energy behind the reforms that were laid down by the Labour Party in our Council manifesto. I mean, good God, *you'd* be the first to complain if I hadn't helped to push through the Abolition of Fares for Old Age Pensioners on London Transport, for instance.

CLIFF: *(Shaking his head in disbelief.)* But, Dad, you told Uncle Tom last night that free-fares for OAPs was just – and I quote – 'a cosmetic job', to cover up the fact that you can't keep your promise about free fares for everyone!

COUNCILLOR: I certainly didn't say it quite like that. What a devious imagination you have. I simply said that it would take much longer than I thought to…well, implement free-fares for everyone.

TOM: *(Smiling.)* Like forever, Councillor?

COUNCILLOR: Now, Tom, you know perfectly well that a politician has to be…pliable to a certain extent in order that his Party can function. I mean, imagine the chaos that we'd have on our hands if every politician tried to inflict his own extreme prejudices on the general public. Not that *my* prejudices are extreme, y'understand. But say they were. Like Enoch Powell's, for instance. Well, I would end up outside my Party, wouldn't I? Like Enoch Powell, to all intents and purposes, is outside his. And then my contribution to society in such a role would be – not unlike Powell's – that of an embittered, rhetorical, racist prophet of doom. I hope some of this is getting through, Cliff.

CLIFF: Are you up to another question, Dad?

COUNCILLOR: Be my guest.

CLIFF: Well, you always *say* that you like helping people…

COUNCILLOR: *(Interrupting.)* I do! It's what I've been elected for. And that's why I'm never at home. I mean, even *you* must be aware, Clifford, that I spend every hour God sends trying to solve the appalling housing problems in East Stratton.

CLIFF: Then why have you avoided getting onto the G.L.C. Housing Committee, then?

COUNCILLOR: *(Choking on his glass of water.)* What a question!

TOM: Isn't it just?

COUNCILLOR: It was a personal decision. Look, Tom, I really don't think the viewers are interested in…

TOM: *(Overriding him.)* Oh but we are.

CLIFF: Is it because of what you told Mum?

COUNCILLOR: Wh-what was that?

CLIFF: Well, you told her… *(Reading.)* 'There's nothing anyone can do about the housing problem in London. And, anyway, tying myself up with lame-duck policies, won't help my career'.

COUNCILLOR: That's a gross exaggeration. I certainly didn't say that…

CLIFF: Sorry, but you *did*, Dad. And then you added; 'London is ungovernable, but one can't shout the truth from the rooftops because it'll only make the public panicky.'

COUNCILLOR: Now just-just a minute!

CLIFF: You also said 'The Labour Party got into the G.L.C. on false pretences by promising reforms that we knew damn well'... *(Looking up from his notes.)* I remember you saying 'damn', Dad. *(Reading.)* ...'That we knew damn well that we couldn't implement even *before* the Elections. Still, it was one of our best campaigns since the Forties.'

COUNCILLOR: Now, Cliff, listen...

CLIFF: Sorry, but I haven't finished yet, Dad. And only last night while we were watching 'Hawaii Five O' you said; 'The Labour Party's nearly as useless as the Tories, and that's really saying something, 'cause the Tories are really useless. There's absolutely nothing to choose between either party. We're both intellectually and morally bankrupt.'

COUNCILLOR: *(Laughing expansively.)* Oh that's funny. No, that's truly very funny.

CLIFF: You weren't laughing when you said it, Dad.

COUNCILLOR: You're quoting me out of context again, son. If you go on like this, you'll get a permanent contract with the BBC. There's nothing they love more than political distortion.

CLIFF: Are you saying that you didn't *say* those things, Dad?

COUNCILLOR: I'm not calling you a liar, son. Not at all. It's just...well, you shouldn't take some of my humorous generalisations about politics so seriously. I mean, for you to imply that I believe that both Parties are...well, are... Well, it's simply absurd. Look, Tom for the sake of the viewers' sanity, I really think that you should ask the questions.

TOM: *(Turning to CLIFF.)* Are there any other policies that your father's concerned with that cause you concern, Cliff?

CLIFF: All of 'em, really. Especially the Ringway System.

COUNCILLOR: The Ringway…?

CLIFF: I just want the truth, Dad, that's all.

COUNCILLOR: If I had any idea that a television company would stoop to…!

TOM: *(Overriding him.)* What about the Ringway System, Cliff?

CLIFF: *(Turning the pages of his pad.)* I'll just check my notes, OK?

COUNCILLOR: Look, the viewers don't pay their licence for this kind of thing.

CLIFF: Ah, here we are! Shall I read it out?

COUNCILLOR: No!

TOM: Yes, please do.

CLIFF: Well, Dad, you said; 'In theory the Labour Party has abandoned'… I think that's the right word. *(Grinning.)* Can hardly read my own writing. Yes, yes, that's right. 'In *theory* the Labour Party has abandoned the Tories' proposed Ringway System, but in *practice* we have approved a Road Widening Scheme. But they're not Motorways – just SIX-LANE HIGHWAYS!' And I remember you laughed rather bitterly when you said that, Dad.

COUNCILLOR: You're determined to have the truth, no matter the cost, aren't you?

CLIFF: Yes. So may I continue? *(COUNCILLOR stares balefully at his son.)* Yes, and you were just as angry when you first explained it, Dad. Because you said that these Six-Laned Highways, with their underpasses, were going to smash right through people's houses, in exactly the same way as the Ringways would have. And, what was worse, you said in five years' time, when the Road Widening Scheme was completed, everyone would suddenly discover – with horror – that the new roads all LINKED UP together, completely encircling London!

TOM: You don't mean Labour's Road Widening Scheme is going to end up just like the Tories' Ringway System?

COUNCILLOR: No, no, no, Tom. You're being simplistic again. You have to realise... I mean, the viewers have to realise that the G.L.C. is not its own master. It's controlled by...

TOM: *(With a cynical smile.)* The Civil Service?

COUNCILLOR: Yes, the Civil Service!

TOM: Oh, not that old chestnut again.

COUNCILLOR: In the same way as the Government is. That's why it's impossible to completely quash a project like the Ringways, or Maplin, because of years of planning under previous Governments. Now everything so bloody computerised that, in reality, a change in the governing body is often only...well, only a change of *faces*!

TOM: But, Councillor, you must have known all this about the Ringway System long before you made your Election pledges. And yet you still had the temerity to promise to abolish the Ringways.

COUNCILLOR: We *have* abolished them! A Road Widening Scheme is not a...well, it's not a Ringway System.

TOM: Now who's playing with words?

COUNCILLOR: We've been a damn sight more successful than the Tories in carrying out our Election prejudices... *(Quickly correcting himself.)* ...promises! I mean, what about Ted Heath's promise to cut prices at a stroke?

CLIFF: His failure doesn't excuse yours, Dad.

COUNCILLOR: If you were in the position of trying to govern, son, you wouldn't be so blissfully sanctimonious. As the Tories have found out to their coast, now they're being undermined by galloping inflation.

CLIFF: I'm not interested in the Tories, Dad. I'm only concerned as to why my father continues to...well, to lie to everyone when you know you can't fulfil even half of your promises!

COUNCILLOR: We don't lie, son. We just…well, voice our hopes outloud, and pray that things will…

TOM: *(Finishing his sentence.)* …Work out. In your favour! Right, Councillor?

COUNCILLOR: Right. And if you had any sense, Mr Bolton, you'd start praying, too.

TOM: Forgive me, Councillor Rennip, but my job is to simply make sure the viewers get the facts and the truth.

COUNCILLOR: Oh not those words again.

CLIFF: He's right to insist on the truth, Dad. How else are we ever to going to…well, progress to a fairer society?

COUNCILLOR: Certainly not by indulging in moral superiority and self-righteousness. And *you're* just as bad, Cliff, making gross accusations, out of what I can only assume is youthful idealism and divine ignorance.

CLIFF: Now, Dad, that's not fair, you're…

COUNCILLOR: *(Overriding him.)* Allow me to finish, please. If you're both as concerned about our nation's welfare, and London in particular, as you say you are; why don't you both get off the critical, hypocritical fence, and join me in the bloody arena? It's the only way you're ever going to come to terms with the fact that politics is *not* an exact science. Be a damn sight simpler if it was. No, politics is like psychiatry in many ways. The practitioners make huge, and often dangerous guesses. Then they use untested drugs, shock treatment, and sometimes lobotomy on the patient – which, in the case of politics, happens to be this country! So all the time we're hoping and praying that we won't go stark-staring-mad during the cure. Yet we know only too well that we *will* go mad without some kind of cure!

CLIFF: Yes, but how do the property speculators fit onto your Freudian couch, Dad? Aren't they due for a lobotomy?

Pause.

COUNCILLOR: Haven't you understood anything I've said?

CLIFF: You've brought me up to believe in specifics, Dad. So I'm leaving the pseudo-psychiatry behind, and asking you a specific question.

COUNCILLOR: Look, why don't you cut out all this Sixth Form arrogance, and try to put yourself in my position for a minute?

CLIFF: I'm supposed to be asking the questions, Dad.

COUNCILLOR: There's no need to be…

CLIFF: Why is it that since you've been on the G.L.C., you haven't done anything to stop the speculators ruining London?

COUNCILLOR: Cliff, will you…?

CLIFF: *(Overriding him.)* Especially when – and I quote; 'Instead of the G.L.C. giving permission to all and sundry to knock up high-rise office blocks, *we* should be building new houses ourselves.'

COUNCILLOR: You're a credit to the KGB. You really are.

CLIFF: What's that supposed to mean?

COUNCILLOR: Because with your expert bugging system, you've already got the answer to your question written down on your pad.

TOM: So why don't you save him the trouble of looking it up, Councillor, and give us *your* answer?

Pause.

COUNCILLOR: *(Grimly.)* You refuse to learn, don't you?

TOM: We just want the plain unvarnished truth as to why the G.L.C. is....

COUNCILLOR: *(Overriding him.)* Alright, alright, I'll give you the godawful truth. And much good will it do you. Or me, for that matter.

CLIFF: *(In his cod American accent.)* OK, so shoot, Dad.

COUNCILLOR: *(After a pause.)* The G.L.C. is broke. That's why.

CLIFF: Oh come on, you can do better than that.

COUNCILLOR: In fact we're so seriously broke that only last November, we adjourned in the middle of a Council meeting – as I'm sure Mr Bolton will recall because the media were there – and we marched over Westminster Bridge to make an official complaint to the Prime Minister. And we informed him that his financial restraints, which he'd put on us, were in fact destroying London. Not that it made any impression on Ted Heath. But then nothing ever does.

CLIFF: You still haven't explained why the speculators have been given the G.L.C.'s blessing to build office blocks in such boroughs as Southwark and Camden, when you should be...

COUNCILLOR: I've just bloody told you! Ted Heath won't *give* us the money to build the houses. And we can't afford to *borrow* the money as the interest rates are so astronomical. So the only way we can get the houses built, as well as keeping all the amenities going, is if we raise the money by increasing the local rates. But unfortunately many of the boroughs, like Southwark and Camden, are very depressed areas, so most of the folk there are on Social Welfare, as a result, the rates are extremely low. This forces the G.L.C. into allowing the speculators to construct high-rise office blocks – because, as you know, the rateable value of office space per square foot is very high. And thus with the accrued revenue, the poorer boroughs can take the strain on their Social Services' bill. Naturally in the process we try to squeeze as many community benefits out of the speculators as possible. In fact before we give them permission to build, generally we ensure that they either make a present of the land, on which *we* can then build houses, known as a Planning Gain, or *they* build us a couple of hundred houses themselves!

TOM: But you never can get anything approaching a fair deal, Councillor. Their profits are far in excess of any…

COUNCILLOR: *(Overriding him.)* There's no need to remind me, Tom. I have to live with it every day. In fact the profits that the speculators are going to cream off Southwark and Camden alone, are greater than the G.L.C.'s entire annual budget.

TOM: Yes, but surely the Government's new measures against speculators will stop all that.

COUNCILLOR: Hm! They'll barely scratch the surface, believe me. No, the land has to be nationalised! Until it is, the profit motive will continue to crucify London.

TOM: You amaze me, Councillor, you really do. You've admitted that speculators are turning London into a concrete tomb. And yet all you do is pontificate, and apologise…

COUNCILLOR: *(Interrupting.)* No, I'm just giving you all the unpleasant truths you've been begging for. We have to face the fact that London is dying! Yes, dying! Why do you think the skilled workers of both the Working *and* Middle Classes are moving to the coast? They're moving because that's where the jobs are. Where the money is. You see, they can no longer afford to live in London. And when you rip the industrious heart out of a city, then that city starts to freeze inside. And there's only one way to bring people back, or at least to provide jobs for those who are unlucky enough to still be here, and that is – and no one's going to like this – we have to capitalise on the one growth industry that we've got left – which happens to be office and commercial work. But first – we have to build the offices. And that means we have to do something that all true liberal thinkers will love; we have to bulldoze through some of our precious history. In fact we have to totally destroy some of London's 19th Century architectural façade.

TOM: But that's an appalling solution, Councillor.

COUNCILLOR: *(With a grim smile.)* Isn't it just? But what other choice have we? With most of the skilled workers gone, we're left with only the Very Rich in Belgravia, plus, of course, the Tourists, and the Very Poor Service Workers elsewhere. Not to mention the Old, the Infirm, the Disabled, the Unemployed, and the Unemployable on Social Welfare. Oh, and of course, we mustn't forget our good friends, the Commuters, who are heavily-subsidised, and who contribute little or nothing to the life blood of London. Except to increase the inordinate congestion on the roads – the Oil Sheikhs permitting, of course – and the monopolising of public transport. In fact the Commuters' only achievement is to rush into town in the morning, and then to rush out even faster at night. That's, of course, if, and when, any trains are running. So if we don't build these 'atrocious' office blocks, and if we don't provide the necessary housing and employment – at whatever cost to the landscape and our historical heritage – very soon we're going to end up as an out-of-work-Venice. Minus the canals. *(A beat.)* Oh don't look so worried, Tom, because we, in the Labour Party, like our despairing accomplices, the Tories, believe in democratic compromise. So we'll only do *half* of what I suggest. And, what's more, you can rely on us to do it half-heartedly. We'll just keep swathing the patient in bandages, and we'll keep on pretending he hasn't got cancer. Poverty will increase, the rich will get richer, and the face of Capitalism will remain respectable – and as heartless as ever – as we slide into the Thames, vigorously waving the tattered flag of Democracy, which, as you know, in Britain's case, is our final defence against any form of genuine progress.

TOM: Thank you very much, Mr Enoch Powell, Prophet of Doom. So how does it feel to be outside your Party?

COUNCILLOR: Well, surely that's what you wanted, isn't it? The death knell.

TOM: No. Just the truth.

COUNCILLOR: Well, now you've got it, what good is it to you? What are you going to do with it? Is it going to change anything? Will it make you, or anyone else, jump into the political arena, and take some real responsibility for once? I very much doubt it. So what useful purpose has this interview served? Other, of course, than worrying the life out of the eight million people who are watching this programme. Though I sincerely hope that most people have had the sense to turn this off. But they probably won't have switched us off because we Brits are internationally famous for our congenital masochism.

TOM: You're so wrong, Councillor. Now we know the truth, there's a vague hope we'll…well, we'll pull ourselves together.

CLIFF: I'm sorry, Dad. Really. I honestly didn't realise that…

COUNCILLOR: It's alright, son. I know you didn't.

CLIFF: Do you think things are really as hopeless as you say…?

COUNCILLOR: I believe that we have been *used*, Cliff!

TOM: You can't shuffle out of it that easily, Councillor.

COUNCILLOR: What a fool I've been! It's so bloody obvious, isn't it?

CLIFF: I don't get you, Dad…

COUNCILLOR: *(Turning on TOM.)* You unmitigated bastard!

TOM: *(With a bland smile.)* Now, now, Councillor, there's no need for abusive language. Remember, you agreed to the experiment.

COUNCILLOR: You sonova...!

TOM: *(Overriding him good-humouredly.)* Yes, well, I think you've made your point. *(The FLOOR MANAGER appears and signals there are 3 minutes to go.)* I'm afraid we'll have to call it an evening now...

COUNCILLOR: No, no! You keep the cameras rolling! *(Shaking his head the FLOOR MANAGER leaves the set.)* I want the viewers to see this through to the finish. You can't just con me into betraying my Party, and then...

TOM: How can the truth be a con, Councillor?

COUNCILLOR: 'Truth'? You don't know what the truth means? You seem to be forgetting that you're nothing but a professional parasite who is living off my fleas!

TOM: *(Calmly.)* Have you finished, Mr Rennip?

COUNCILLOR: You smug, unfeeling little... But then you've every right to be smug, haven't you? Because your achievements tonight are unparalleled even by your dubious standards. Well, let's face it, in thirty minutes you've tried – and, what's more, you've probably succeeded – in torpedoing my entire life's work. Not to mention what you've done to my son. Just look at his face! Could we have it in Ultra Close Up, please? 'Cause it's going to be a helluva long time before you trust me again, Cliff, isn't it? *(A beat.)* Isn't it? *(CLIFF looks away.)* If ever. *(The COUNCILLOR jabs his finger at TOM.)* And yet it's you, Bolton, who should've been on trial tonight!

TOM: Trial? There's been no trial, Councillor. So, for once, why don't you be completely honest with everyone, and admit that you came here to do a P.R. job on yourself? But unfortunately for you, your son forced you out into the open. So if you've been struck down by lightning, it's lightning of your own making. And, what's more, I believe there's part of you that *wanted* to spill the beans. You see, because a man of your intelligence never does anything without an ulterior motive. I'll go further; I think you even enjoyed it.

COUNCILLOR: *(Standing up.)* You coming, Cliff? *(CLIFF doesn't move, so the COUNCILLOR turns to the camera.)* Well, thank you for your indulgence, ladies and gentlemen. I hope you can all see what has happened here tonight. Because you have all been conned, too. So now I'd like to leave you with one crucial question. If London is to be saved – and I only say if – who will save it? The so-called Truth Seekers? Or the Politicians?

The COUNCILLOR leaves the set.

TOM: *(To Camera.)* Well, that's about it for this series. And as I said before we started, tonight's programme would – at the very least – be unpredictable. And like Councillor Rennip, I would like to leave you all with one final question, which I regard as being even more important than 'the saving of London'. And my question concerns Democracy itself. If our Democracy is to be saved – and I only say if – who will save it. The Politicians? Or the Truth-Seekers? Goodnight.

Closing music. Then excitedly the FLOOR MANAGER reappears.

FLOOR MANAGER: My God, Tom, that was really fantastic!

TOM: *(Staring at the dazed, silent figure of CLIFF.)* Was it?

FLOOR MANAGER: Yeah, they absolutely love it up there! *(Listening through his cans.)* What? They say they've never seen such pain and embarrassment in all their… *(He trails off as he realises what he has said.)* Marvellous! They say it was marvellous! You alright, Tom?

TOM: *(Going over to CLIFF.)* But it's what you wanted, Cliff, isn't it?

CLIFF doesn't answer.

FLOOR MANAGER: They're really jumping up and down up there! Terrific!

TOM: Cliff, I only did what we…agreed…

FLOOR MANAGER: Boy oh boy! That was real television. Beautiful!

TOM: Cliff…

FLOOR MANAGER: Just beautiful!

Slow fade.

The End.

SHAKEBAG
A COMEDY IN ONE ACT

Characters

CHRISTABEL

JO

BEATRICE

MARTIN

ROD

BILL

Shakebag was first performed at the Soho Poly, London on 10th May 1976 with the following cast;

CHRISTABEL, Catherine Griller

JO, Jean Fergusson

MARTIN, Paul Hastings

BEATRICE, Clare Richards

ROD, Ronald Fernee

BILL, Peter Pacey

Director, Ian Lindsay

Designer, Harry Duffin

The stage of the Romeo Amateur Dramatic Society.

Time; April 23, Shakespeare's Birthday.

On the stage there are six chairs, a table, several discarded pieces of scenery and a toolkit. Also there is a side table with a kettle, mugs, tea-caddy, teaspoons, a radio, a rack of CDs, and a very large overflowing prop-basket, which is filled with swords etc.

Off, we hear the ACTORS talking and laughing.

Then CHRISTABEL, in her early 20s, who is pretty with an infectious giggle, enters, singing to herself.

CHRISTABEL: 'When that I was and a tiny little boy,
　　　With hey, ho, the wind and the rain,
　　　A foolish thing was but a toy,
　　　For the rain it raineth every day.'

JO, the director, who is in her late 30s, and always appears to be under stress, enters with her briefcase over her shoulder. She has an unlit cigarette butt in her mouth, and she is clapping.

CHRISTABEL: Like it?

JO: No, sounds terrible.

CHRISTABEL: Oh I thought it was the perfect way to kick off Shakespeare's birthday.

JO: Yes, but with that mob out there about to get their gnashers into his works, it's not surprising that the Bard also decided to drop dead on April 23rd. *(Calling off.)* Oh come on, cast, get your codpieces in here. 'Cause soon it'll be time to finish before we've even started. *(Rummaging through her briefcase.)* Oh God, I've forgotten the First Folio again. Beatrice, bless her academic socks, will have my guts for pantie-hose. *(Shouting.)* Oh do pull your fingers out, guys. Just because we have a private bar here, it doesn't mean you have to drink it dry.

CHRISTABEL: *(Offering JO a mouth-spray.)* Want a squirt?

JO: Is my breath that bad, then?

CHRISTABEL: No, I adore the smell of garlic. Even second hand. *(After squirting it into her own mouth.)* But I always find a couple of quick squirts saves a lot of embarrassment when I go into my Lady Macbeth steamed-up-clinches.

JO: I'm sure these Gauloise don't help. 'Fact when I woke up this morning, my tongue felt like a tobacco plantation in high summer. That's why I've not even lit it this morning. *(She drops her cigarette butt into a bin as she calls off.)* Listen, you guys, *Macbeth* and *The Dream* have need of you, so pull your digits out!

MARTIN, who is in his 30s, and who is the only professional actor in the group, enters, puffing his pipe and clutching his Guinness. He is carrying a backpack.

JO: I wasn't, of course, referring to your digit, Mark!

MARTIN: Oh. I was half hoping you were.

CHRISTABEL: *(Indicating MARTIN's pipe.)* Mmmm. What a wondrous aroma.

MARTIN: *(Pipe business.)* Elizabethan Shag. And they certainly did a lot of that. But, of course, it could be Raleigh's Rubbed Flake. Can never remember. But don't worry, Jo, I won't smoke in here.

He taps out his pipe. Then he puts it away in his backpack, and pulls out a newspaper.

BEATRICE: *(Off.)* Mark! Mark!

BEATRICE, who is a donnish woman in her sixties, complete with spectacles and a briefcase, enters. She is cradling a large gin and tonic.

BEATRICE: Mark, are you, indeed, seriously attempting to make a rational parallel between Macbeth's 'shard-borne beetle' and Leontes' metaphorical 'spider', in that passage where 'he cracks his gorge, his sides, with violent hefts'?

MARTIN: 'Oh I have drunk and seen the spider.'

BEATRICE: Forgive me, but there you go again, Mark, with your congenitally-sloppy thinking. You destroyed the rhythm of the line by adding that 'O'.

MARTIN: What 'O'?

BEATRICE: Not the French painter! No, I'm referring to that unnecessary exclamatory vowel that you inserted before 'I have drunk and seen the spider'.

JO: *(To CHRISTABEL.)* Oh dear God, we're in for another terrible session.

MARTIN: *(Looking up from his newspaper.)* Talking of 'sessions', Jo, can you give me a sub on my fee?

JO: I'm sorry but I don't have the petty cash to hand at the moment, Mark, but as soon as we've finished, I'll… *(Trailing off.)* Chrissy, why are you staring at me like that?

CHRISTABEL: I've just remembered that Mr Smallicott, the chief librarian, has told me to tell you that you still have five books overdrawn. And if you don't return them within the week, he's going to start legal proceedings against you.

JO: He can start all the rotten proceedings he likes! I need those books for the Lower Sixth for the rest of this rotten term, so I'm hanging onto them. OK? *(Groaning MARTIN sits on a chair.)* Yes, do sit down, everyone. *(To the censorious figure of BEATRICE.)* Or stand, if you prefer it. *(CHRISTABEL, who is still sulking at having been reprimanded, lies down on the stage.)* Yes, you can even lie down, Chrissy, if you deem it absolutely necessary. Right! So now I'd like to kick-off by… Where the hell is Rod?

CHRISTABEL: Last time I saw him, he was heading for the loo.

MARTIN: Yes, Yanks just can't hold British bitter, can they? Mind, it's not surprising because in L.A. all you get is fizzy gnat's pee.

ROD, who is a lanky American in his 20s, ambles in.

ROD: Sorry about that, folks. Hope I've not kept you waiting too long.

JO: You've not been that much worse than anyone else, Rodney. Bill seems to have got lost, too. So why don't you pull up a pew? *(To everyone.)* Right, now we've all had a nice long drink, and we're all fairly relaxed, I thought we'd just have an investigatory chat tonight. And as this is the first time that Mark, our sole professional actor, has subjected himself to working with us, I thought I'd start by exploring…

MARTIN: *(Interrupting her.)* Talking of 'subs', Joe, you won't forget mine, will you?

JO: 'Course not.

MARTIN: I'm only here for the beer, y'know.

JO: Quite. Now as we have only the principals here tonight – plus, of course, the Society's secretary, Beatrice, who is also our very knowledgeable Shakespearean advisor – it seems the perfect opportunity for us to explore intellectually, and conceptually, the *raison d'être* for doing *Macbeth* and *A Midsummer Night's Dream* in repertoire, so… *(She trails off when she sees that CHRISTABEL is convulsed with laughter.)* I didn't think I'd uttered anything particularly witty, Chrissy.

CHRISTABEL: *(Still lying on the stage, and laughing and kicking her heels.)* You haven't!

BEATRICE: I second that.

JO: So what's your problem, Chrissy?

CHRISTABEL: *(Laughing even louder.)* Nothing! Nothing at all!

(CHRISTABEL is lying next to MARTIN, so she tweaks his ankle, while she laughs and points at ROD. Momentarily MARTIN looks mystified, and then he, too, roars with laughter.)

ROD: *(Mystified.)* What…well, what the hell have I done now?

MARTIN: *(Camply.)* It's more a matter of what you *haven't* done, sweetie. *(Perplexed ROD stands up while MARTIN points at ROD's crotch, and we see ROD's fly-zipper is undone.)* Ooooh…!'Is this a dagger, which I see before me? The handle towards my hand. Come, let me clutch thee!'

ROD: *(Struggling with his zipper.)* Oh Jesus save me!

MARTIN: 'I have thee not, and yet I see thee still!'

ROD: Oh God help me, the zip's stuck! I think it's come off its fucking runner!

BEATRICE: Language!

ROD: *(Covering his crotch with his hands.)* Oh sorry.

MARTIN: *(Advancing on ROD, with an extended arm.)*
'Art thou not, fatal vision, sensible
To feel as to sight, or art thou but
A dagger of the mind, a false creation
Proceeding from the heat-oppressed brain?'

General laughter and applause.

ROD: Stop laughing, everyone! What the hell am I gonna do?

MARTIN: *(In cod American.)* Go get yerself some pliers. I always find they work wonders.

ROD: Why do I need pliers?

CHRISTABEL: So you can yank your zip up, silly, and protect your willy.

JO: *(Pointing.)* And you're bound to find some in Bill's toolkit. So now can we get on, please?!

(CHRISTABEL rummages around in BILL's toolkit.)

ROD: *(With his hands over his crotch.)* Jesus, it's so goddam embarrassing!

CHRISTABEL: *(Now waving a pair of pliers at him.)* Ooooh! Can I have the first yank?

ROD: *(Taking the pliers from her.)* No, you screwing can't! So far I've only lost my modesty. Christ knows what I'd lose if you started jerking these pincers around my groin.

ROD crosses the stage with the pliers.

JO: Now *where* d'you think you're going, Rod?

ROD: To the John, where else? Yanking is a very intimate business. *(Everyone laughs.)* What I mean is… Oh God!

ROD exits to more laughter. Only BEATRICE is not amused.

JO: Right, now let's get on before anything else goes pear-shaped…

But JO is drowned by a loud flourish on the drums as BILL, the Cockney carpenter-cum-general factotum, enters from the opposite side of the stage, with a drum around his neck, which he is beating with two sticks. Also he is chewing gum vigorously.

BILL: 'Are we all met?'

JO: Well, that's highly debatable.

BILL: 'Are we all met?'

BEATRICE: Feeling feverish, William?

BILL: No, I aint! And if you weren't so ignorant, Bea, you'd know that 'Are we all met?' is Bottom's first line! *(Everyone laughs.)* So wot's the towrag joke?

JO: Now don't get yourself in a paddy, Bill. See, we haven't even started discussing the plays yet. Never mind actually rehearsing them.

BILL: Look, it aint my fault the poncey vicar dropped you all in it, is it? Well, Mister Dog-Collar was s'pposed to give you *'is* Bottom, wasn't he? An' because 'e's gone an' done a runner back to 'is flock, you've now got to put up wiv *my* Bottom, ent you? An' I'm just the crappy carpenter around 'ere, so I've never done no actin' before, 'ave I?

Well, certainly nuffink written by Old Misery-Guts-Will-Shakebag!

BEATRICE: William, please! You must stop casting aspersions on the beauteous Bard of Avon. Especially on his much-revered birthday!

BILL: Well, as long as you lot realise that I'm only exposin' my talents to the hoipoloi, to prevent the Romeo Amateur Dramatic Society from endin' up on the slagheap! – where, by rights, it belongs!

CHRISTABEL: *(To MARTIN, who has his eyes closed, and who gives a little snore.)* Mark, I do believe you've fallen asleep.

MARTIN: Oh…have I?

BILL: So if you'd rather call in some actor-bus-conductor, or a big-mouth-dustman to knock orf '*is* bleeding Bottom, well, I, for one, will be cruddin' relieved!

CHRISTABEL: Oh, Billy, Billy! Will you stop being a silly-billy?

JO: Yes, Bill, because, of course, we want you to give us your bleeding Bottom. *(Quickly correcting herself.)* I mean, of course, your plain Bottom.

MARTIN: *(Aside to CHRISTABEL.)* Yes, and I just can't wait to see him with his asses' head on.

BILL: Hey, watch it, mister! Just 'cause you're the only pro round 'ere, there's no need for you to get all smart-arsey, uppity and hoity-toity!

MARTIN yawns as he puts his newspaper over his face.

JO: Bill, will you please mind your ps and qs?! You must realise that Mark is doing us the greatest favour by coming down here to give his Macbeth and Oberon.

BILL: If '*e's* doin you a favour? Wot the 'ell d'you fink *I'm* doin'?

JO: Oh, for pity's sake, clam up, Bill, and let's get on!

BILL: Right, you've arsked for it, Jo. I'm goin' to sit 'ere, an' 'ave an 'Ollywood sulk!

BEATRICE: Could I say something?

JO: In a minute, Beatrice. But now we must surge forward!

BEATRICE: But this is important.

JO: Oh Beatrice, please, allow me to…

BEATRICE: *(Overriding her.)* No, I'm sorry but I don't approve of any of the numerous cuts that Mark is proposing in the latter half of *Macbeth.* The play is short enough as it is!

JO: Yes, I'm sure you're right, Beatrice, but now let's get…

MARTIN: *(Interrupting.)* What d'you mean she's right? I always play the Scottish gentleman with those cuts. In fact I may have to cut a lot more. Especially on the peanuts you're paying me.

JO: You'll get your sub after we've finished, for Christ's sake! *(Embarrassed by her outburst.)* Look, I'm sorry, Mark, but with all the time everyone's wasted drinking tonight, it's not left us very much of the evening to do anything. So I just want to say a few well-chosen words…

ROD returns, flourishing the pliers.

ROD: I've done it. After several yanks, my codpiece has zipped up a treat!

JO: Jolly good. Now will you please close your legs. *(Quickly.)* What I mean is, will you just sit down, so I can…?

ROD: Trouble is, I got my shirt stuck in the zipper in the process, but…if I keep crossing my legs, there's a slim chance the zipper'll hold out for the rest of the rehearsal.

JO: Which is more than *I* will, if we don't have some instant hush! *(BILL snatches the pliers from ROD, and puts them in his tool bag.)* So now we've finished with the zipping and yanking, I'd like to start by saying a few well-chosen about the *raison d'être* for doing *Macbeth* and *A Midsummer Night's...*

CHRISTABEL: (*Overriding her, and whispering loudly to MARTIN.*) You're going to be absolutely super as Macbeth, Martin. And I just can't wait for our intimate scenes together.

JO: Chrissy, please do put a sock in it!

CHRISTABEL: I'm sorry, Jo, but it's very important for our theatrical chemistry that Martin realises how much I'm looking forward to all our steamy scenes together. *(To MARTIN.)* Because, you see, I'll need all the tips you can give me. Oh don't worry, Martin, I'm very good at verse-speaking. 'Fact I got the top prize at school. Also I look quite raunchy in historical costumes...

JO: (*Interrupting.*) Oh for God's sake, Christabel!

CHRISTABEL: Well, I do! Our drama teacher, Mr Large, said my Antigone had incredible sexual authority, and, on occasions, even 'sensual nobility'. Indeed, so much so, that every night of our run, I could see that Mr Large was dying to leap onto the stage and gobble my appendages! *(Giggling.)* But my only hang-up is I do have a terrible problem with my First Night nerves.

BILL: Oh Jesus wept!

JO: Yes, and I'm going to start weeping soon.

CHRISTABEL: No, seriously, Jo, my First Night nerves are a thing to behold! 'Fact the moment the curtain goes up, and I'm Centre Stage with my crown on, then - hey presto - my left thigh starts shaking. Look...see! *(Demonstrating.)* Yes, there it goes! And it's always the left one. And – as you can hear - I haven't even uttered one of the Bard's immortal lines yet. But the truth is, I only have to *think* about the First Night, and instantly I turn into an elongated blancmange!

JO: Oh, Chrissy, do you really have to keep shaking your left thigh like that?

CHRISTABLE: It's alright for *you*, Jo. 'Cause on the first night, when I'm doing my quivering-blancmange-routine, you'll just be sitting in the back-row of the Stalls, clapping like billyo. While *I'll* be the one who's critically-crucified-alive because of my left shaking thigh. So, for everyone's sake, I hope that when I'm in my Lady M's slinky gear, it won't show too much. See, sometimes my thigh shakes so incredibly, I feel as if I've got St. Vitus Dance.

ROD: Like now, for instance?

CHRISTABEL: That's a very mean thing to say, Rod. Look, see…I can barely stand!

MARTIN: *(Crossing over to her and physically supporting her.)* Oh don't worry your pretty little head, honey. I'll always be here to hold you up. When I'm awake, that is. And, more importantly, if and when I get paid. *(Intimately he puts his arm around her waist. Then he turns her towards him.)* See, sweet lips…you can really rely on me.

CHRISTABEL: *(Enjoying the moment.)* OOOhhh…thank you, Martin. And I promise I'll make it up to you on the Second Night.

MARTIN: Then I can't wait 'till the Curtain's down, and we're back at my place. Yes, yes, baby doll, you just keep looking into my eyes like that…and it's going to be one magically-erogenous moment after another.

JO: 'Erogenous'?! Oh Heaven help us! Look, Mark, please! Can I just say a few well-chosen……?

MARTIN: *(Overriding her, to CHRISTABEL.)* And it won't even matter if you dry stone dead, honeybunch. Macbeth will never fail you. *(BEATRICE snorts derisively.)* Oh c'mon, Beatrice, surely we're friends now? Well, I thought our quotation-swapping-session, over all those drinks you bought me, was very intellectually revealing.

BEATRICE: *(Dryly.)* It certainly was.

JO: Look, when you've all finished, perhaps I can…

BEATRICE: It's just a pity that you didn't always quote the Bard correctly, Mark.

MARTIN: Oh, didn't I?

BEATRICE: No. You see, Hamlet does not say – as you made him say; 'O, that this too, too *solid* flesh would melt.'

Groaning MARTIN leans back in his chair puts his newspaper over his head.

JO: We're not even doing *Hamlet*!

BILL: Oh stroll on. 'Ere we go again!

BILL starts hammering.

JO: What the devil are you doing, Bill? You're making things infinitely worse!

BILL: *(Hammering.)* I'm just enjoying meself. Like everyone else. D'you mind?

ROD: *(Laughing and clapping BILL's hammering efforts.)* Atta boy, atta boy!

BEATRICE: *(Shouting above the hammering.)* You see, Mark – *(To the others.)* – and this is also of the utmost importance for the rest of you! – by your saying; 'too, too *solid* flesh', well, that implies that Hamlet is overweight, and that he is, in fact, a fatty! Indeed, it makes him sound as if he's a Renaissance Billy Bunter!

ROD claps and laughs even louder, while JO bangs her fists on the table as she tries to silence ROD's clapping and BILL's hammering.)

JO: Will everyone please belt up, and listen to me?!

BILL: I can't belt up an' listen to you, 'cause I'm buildin' the bloomin' set! *(Taking the pliers out of his tool bag and throwing them to ROD.)* 'Ere! Now you put these to decent use for once, and pull them nails outta that plonkin' plank.

JO: Oh for pity's sake, Billy! How the hell can you build the set, when we haven't even decided yet what set we want builded? I mean, of course 'building'!

BILL: *(Hammering.)* Then you'll have to make up yer mind damn smartish, won't you?

BEATRICE: *(Who has been speaking continuously throughout.)* Whereas by using the words 'too, too *sullied* flesh', Mark – which is what Shakespeare actually wrote – we become aware that, in reality, Hamlet is contemplating suicide because he regards his 'sullied' corporeal body as having contaminated the world in general, and Denmark in particular.

JO: *(Who is now furiously pounding on BILL's drum with no authority whatsoever.)* Silence! Silence! I will have SODDING SILENCE!

MARTIN: *(Winking at JO, who is suddenly embarrassed by what she has just said.)* Very impressive, Josephine. Really.

BEATRICE: *(Continuing unabashed.)* Which only goes to prove that the live performance of Shakespeare on the stage is a complete waste of time.

ROD: *(Laughing.)* Outta sight, Bea. That's just too cool!

BEATRICE: I'm being perfectly serious, Rodney. Nothing spoils the Bard more than a group of enthusiastic actors tearing into him! *(General laughter. Nodding vigorously BEATRICE points at them all derisively.)* See! See! My very point. You're all the same, and you're all to blame! Because you miss all the subtle Elizabethan shades of meaning. Indeed, none of you 'thespians' are intelligent enough to understand, and then to elucidate, the derivations of the words that you're raucously mouthing.

MARTIN: *(With an ironic smile.)* Does that also include frustrated, would-be, spinster closet-thespians like your good self?

BEATRICE: Sticks and stones may break my bones, but puerile words will never hurt me. You see, Mark, I know the truth. And the truth is, Shakespeare is first and foremost a philosophical and social poet, who should only be read. And outloud, if you deem it absolutely necessary. But his sacred words should only be articulated to oneself, alone, and in the private confines of one's home. Especially on his birthday!

JO: Oh for God's sake, Beatrice, please go back to the bar and get yourself another double gin. And as long as you stay there for at least a couple of minutes, you can put your gin on my tossing tab.

MARTIN: *(Handing BEATRICE his glass.)* Yes, and while you're at it, Professor, you can freshen this up with another Guinness. There's a darling.

BEATRICE: As for your idea, Jo, of you directing *Macbeth* and *A Midsummer Night's Dream* at the same time, and in tandem, and then performing them together in repertoire – well, it's not only gruesomely gimmicky, it's serial sacrilege. In fact, it's much worse. It's like playing Beethoven's Fifth in the middle of Brahm's Lullaby! *(ROD hums the Fifth while CHRISTABEL sings the Lullaby, and this almost reduces BEATRICE to tears.)* You may well mercilessly mock my scholarship, but it does not alter one iota…

JO: *(Overriding her.)* Beatrice, for God's sake, put a blue stocking in it, will you? Look, I know I foolishly said that we would conduct these rehearsals in a democratic manner – i.e.; anyone can shove their oar in whenever they like – but I still feel that I, as the purported director, should be allowed to open the proceedings before we start laying all the bleeding oars around each other's bleeding heads! *(For a moment there is silence.)* Good. Now I'd like to start by giving you all a brief run-down about the dual concepts involved in… *(She trails off to address BEATRICE, who is now tearfully crossing the stage with the two glasses.)* Oh Beatrice, those aren't real tears by any chance, are they?

BEATRICE: *(Sobbing.)* When you're all prepared to listen to… well, to someone who's devoted her very…insignificant life to researching the profound depths of the greatest artist who's ever lived, then you can find her…in the Snug Bar. But, Jo, you did say I could put a triple gin on your tab, didn't you?

JO: *(Gulping.)* Triple?

MARTIN: Yes, and don't forget my pint of Guinness.

Nodding and sobbing BEATRICE exits.

JO: *(Calling after her.)* Beatrice, look, I really didn't mean to upset you, but… Well, I *am* supposed to be the director, so I should be allowed to say the odd word occasionally. *(BILL raises his hammer.)* Oh Bill, please don't start all that hammering again!

CHRISTABEL: Ugh…this all so tedious.

JO goes into a coughing fit.

BILL: *(To JO.)* So wot you decided on, then? Pillars, doors, steps, platforms, windows? Or the whole ruddy lot? As per-ruddy-usual.

ROD: *(As he pats the coughing JO on her back.)* Look, Jo, you told us that you haven't had a fag since last night, but the truth is, you should never smoke again , 'cause it's…

JO: *(Interrupting and coughing.)* I know, I know, it's killing me. But I still should have brought the rest of my ciggies with me because when one's authority is totally undermined – like *mine* is! – well, what the hell else is there left?

BILL: Well, we've still got a couple of old thrones left from our last theatrical cock-up. Yeah, and for good measure, I can also throw in the odd – and it *is* a very odd – arch, if you like.

JO: Look, at present I don't know what I want in the way of sodding scenery! You see, Bill, first we've got to decide what style we're doing the plays in, and in what period. So if you'll all just allow me a few well-chosen words about the *raison d'être* for doing *The Dream* and *Macbeth* in tandem…

(CHRISTABEL groans audibly while MARTIN snores as BEATRICE returns with her gin.)

BEATRICE: *(Prodding the sleeping MARTIN.)* They've run out of Guinness.

MARTIN: *(Waking.)* Buggeration!

JO: Yes, but in a way, I must say that *you* are right, Rod.

ROD: *(Surprised.)* I am?

JO: About what you said in the bar. Because, it's true, there is a surprising common denominator to *The Dream* and *Macbeth.*

BEATRICE: Yes, in your nightmares, there is.

JO: No, Beatrice. Rod put his finger on it – not literally, of course – when he said that *Macbeth* and *The Dream* are both inherently… *(Coyly.)* …'sexy'.

CHRISTABEL: *(Suddenly interested.)* Really?

JO: Yes, you see, they're both riddled with the Supernatural, which we all know is a very 'sexy' subject indeed, so….

BEATRICE: *(Interrupting as she crosses herself.)* So I think it's time for another gin. But I do wish their lemons didn't always have mould on 'em.

BEATRICE exits.

JO: *(Calling after her.)* But, Beatrice, surely even *you* agree that the Supernatural forms part of the infrastructure of both plays? *(BILL does a brief threatening patter on his drums while ROD provides a spooky accompaniment on his recorder/guitar.)*

Thank you, gents. No, really. 'Cause it is nice to know that our carpenter and our Transatlantic travel agent can be relied upon to provide all the required sound effects.

BILL: I'm also providin' me bleedin' Bottom! Don't forget that. Not to mention makin' the char. *(Plugging in the kettle.)* Anyone care for a cuppa?

CHRISTABEL: Oh yes, please, Billy! There's nothing like something hot for calming my thigh.

(General laughter.)

MARTIN: *(Emerging from behind his newspaper.)* Listen, Jo, don't you think we should dispense with all this introductory chat, and just get down to some real work…

JO: *(Overriding him.)* No, no! *(Struggling with another coughing fit.)* It's…most important…that we…finish discussing…my concept…

MARTIN: *(Patting her back.)* I still don't see how your concept of the Supernatural is going to help us plot the two plays.

JO: *(Slowly recovering.)* Yes, but the…Supernatural is very… with-it today, isn't it? That's why it's imperative that we should bring it to the fore in our productions.

MARTIN: Yes, Joe, but we can do all that while we're actually working on the text…

JO: *(Interrupting.)* No, we can't! Magic is at the hub of both plays. *(Coughing again.)* You see, *Macbeth* is bulging with witches, and *The Dream* is absolutely packed full of fairies!

BILL: A bit like the Actin' Profession. Milk, everybody?

MARTIN: Yes, but I think she's only referring to the variety with rainbow wings and twitching antennae.

BILL: Like I said, a bit like the Actin' Profession. Sugar, Chrissy?

CHRISTABLE: Oh, no sugar, thank you. But lashings of milk, please, Bill.

JO: Look, for God's sake, will everyone pay attention? Well, it's all getting totally out of hand again!

ROD: So what's new?

JO: Now to get back to my point, Martin. On the one hand, with *The Dream,* and its flitting fairies, we'll be giving the audience all the magic that…well, that *Peter Pan* has got, and more. And on the other hand, with *Macbeth,* and its diabolical witches, we'll show them the reverse malefic side of the occult coin. Right?

MARTIN: Yes, I suppose, when I'm playing the Scottish gent, I could bring out all the satanic imagery. *(Instantly he becomes MACBETH.)*
'Now o'er the one half world
Nature seems dead, and wicked dreams abuse
The curtain'd sleep; witchcraft celebrates
Pale Hecate's offerings, and wither'd murder
Alrum'd by his sentinel, the wolf,
Whose howl's his watch, thus – with his stealthy pace,
With Tarquin's ravishing strides, towards his design
Moves like a ghost.'

(A beat. Then, with a smug smile, MARTIN sits down again and closes his eyes. He is bored by his own brilliance.)

CHRISTABEL: *(Clapping enthusiastically.)* Wow! 'Fact double wow, Mark! That really chills the blood, doesn't it?

BEATRICE: *(Reappearing with her replenished gin.)* Not from here, it doesn't.

BILL: *(Waving the kettle.)* Cuppa, Bea?

BEATRICE: And dilute the gin? *(In her best French accent.)* *Impossible*!

MARTIN: *(To BEATRICE.)* So, *mademoiselle*, what - in your 'ever-so-umble' opinion - was wrong with my exquisite delivery?

JO: Oh bloody hell! Do we have to?

BEATRICE: Absolutely. Because Mark should have made much more of 'Tarquin's ravishing strides'. You see, it's of the utmost importance that the untutored audience realise that Shakespeare was referring to his early poem; *The Rape of Lucrece,* in which, as you know, the General Tarquin…

ROD: *(Interrupting.)* …Rapes Lucrece!

BEATRICE: Quite.

JO: Right, so now we've all had our little Roman orgy, could we please get on?

ROD: *(To BILL.)* No milk for me, thanks.

BILL: Ugh! These tea-bags are disgustin'.

JO: Bill, just shut the fuck up, will you!? *(Quickly.)* What I mean is that…we're all agreed that we will stress the Supernatural and the Black Arts in our productions. Right?

MARTIN: Yes, I suppose *Macbeth* could be regarded as a combination of Bram Stoker and Dennis Wheatley in verse.

ROD: Yeah, but why don't we do it more like…well more like a stage version of *The Wicker Man*?

BILL: Ugh! Wot an 'orrible thought!

BEATRICE: *(Smiling.)* Oh I don't know. Setting Mark on fire might hot things up a bit.

MARTIN: *(Returning her smile.)* Saint Joan also went up in flames. *(Pointedly to BEATRICE.)* And she was a virgo intacto spinster, too.

JO: Sometimes being here is worse than being in Hell.

BILL: *(Waving a cup.)* So, Jo, d'you want it weak or strong? Not that it'll make much difference.

JO: Weak. I mean…I don't want any blasted tea! *(To everyone.)* Look, why are you all just sitting there 'Like patience on a monument grinning at grief'? *(To BEATRICE.)* Yes, I know Willy Shakebag didn't write that. But now that we've agreed to go ahead with my multi-faceted Supernatural concept, we need to explore how…

CHRISTABEL: *(Interrupting as she retouches her makeup.)* Look, I'm sorry, Jo, but I thought these were going to be fun-productions. Like we used to do at school. *(Giggling.)* When I was the Third Witch on the left.

JO: *(Fighting through another coughing fit.)* God in…Heaven, what have I…done to…deserve this?

MARTIN: *(Waving his pipe.)* You should try puffing on a pipe sometime. It's marginally better on the lungs. And it would suit you more.

JO: *(Almost choking.)* Charming!

CHRISTABEL: *(Giving her Third Witch)*
'Where shall we three meet again,
In thunder lightning or in rain.

BEATRICE: 'When the hurly-burly's done,
When the battle's lost and won.

ROD: 'Where the place?

MARTIN: 'Upon the heath.

CHRISTABEL: 'There to meet with…MAC*BEETH*!'

General laughter.

JO: That's it! That is bloody it! *(Going.)* I can't take any fornicating more!

BILL: Sure you don't want a cuppa?

JO: No! I just want a very long…LEAK!

JO exits.

CHRISTABEL: It's true, though, isn't it? *Macbeth's* got so many gorgeous comic possibilities. What with Banquo's Ghost getting his cloak caught on a nail at the banqueting table. Then when he tries to disappear, Banquo's Ghost accidentally pulls all the platters and beer-mugs onto the floor with a huge clatter.

CHRISTABEL collapses in a fit of giggles.

BILL: Yeah, well, I once saw a production in Clapham, and when Birnam Wood came to Dunsinane, I remember Macduff's boys troopin' onto the stage in their tartan kilts, and they was wavin' their Christmas trees in one 'and, and they was jigging their sporrans up an' down in the other.

CHRISTABEL: *(Giggling.)* Yeah, it's all too hysterical for words, isn't it?

MARTIN: You bet ya. 'Fact I had a similar experience when I was giving my Scottish gent at the Glasgow Cits. And just as I was about to come on with; 'They have tied me to a stake, I cannot fly', to my amazement, I saw that Old Siward was tottering around the stage, trying to stick his beard back on. But instead of him saying – *(In his old man's doddering voice.)* 'Do we but find the tyrant's power tonight, Let us be beaten if we cannot fight.' – the old codger – whose name now escapes me – was so busy trying to stick his beard back on that he completely messed up, and instead he said – *(In his old man's voice.)*
'Do we but find the…*pirate's tower…today*,
We will be beaten, or we'll…RUN AWAY'!

More laughter as JO returns.

JO: *(Ironic.)* Very droll, Mark, very droll. But I still don't see how it helps us to resolve all our conceptual problems, and…

MARK: Look, if we start to rehearse one of the plays, Jo – as I'm constantly advocating – then, more than likely, all the problems will start resolving and solving themselves.

JO: OK, OK. Point taken. *(To everyone's amazement, she starts to draw a vast chalk circle in the middle of the stage.)* So we will commence….by setting *Macbeth* inside…a huge pentacle. And it will be somewhat… like…this. And in the middle… of this pentacle…you will do…all your soliloquies, Mark.

BILL: Wot the 'Ell's a pissin' pentacle?

BEATRICE: *(Now somewhat squiffy because of all her gins.)* It's King Solomon's six-pointed star in a circle, which witches and warlocks use for occult ceremonies, in order to raise up spiritual revenants, ghosts and poltergeists… *(Slurring her words.)* …etcetera…etcetera… Or if a warlock is feeling particularly adventurous, he can raise up Old Nick Himself!

CHRISTABEL giggles.

ROD: *(Following JO around as she continues to create her pentacle with chalk.)* Gee, Jo! This pentacle's a brilliant concept.

JO: Thank you, Rodney. I'm glad someone appreciates the product of all my sleepless nights.

(BEATRICE drifts into the chalk circle, and unsteadily she practice some witch-like gestures. Then she emits a witch's cackle.)

BEATRICE: Yes…veritably…vis-à-vis your pentacle…you may have the seeds of an idea here, Joe. But it's your *only* idea, mind.

JO: *(Still labouring over the pentacle.)* Thanks a bunch.

BEATRICE: No, it is an indisputable fact that Shakespeare and his fellow Elizabethans were profoundly frightened of witches.

BILL: *(As he starts to saw a plank.)* Well, thanks for the first clunkin' clue.

JOE: So what are you sawing that up for?

MARTIN: What, indeed?

BILL: Well, wotever else you'll want in the way of scenery, you're obviously gonna need three stakes to burn the witches at the end of *Macbeth,* ent you?

JO: God Almighty!

BILL: I don't fink 'E comes into it much.

CHRISTABEL: *(Pulling a CD out of her handbag.)* No, what we need…is atmosphere.

CHRISTABEL puts a CD in the stereo.

JO: Chrissy, what d'you think you're doing?

CHRISTABEL: I brought some music along in case we reached an impasse. And I think we have.

MARTIN: So are you going to do a striptease to it, sweet lips, to liven things up?

ROD: *(Laughing.)* Yeah, what sorta music is it, Chrissy? *(He crosses over to her, but while ROD's picking up the CD label, he knocks BILL's tea over.)* Oh fuck a duck! I'm sorry, but it just isn't my day.

BILL: *(Throwing ROD a rag.)* Here! Mop it up with this.

CHRISTABEL: *(Waving her forefinger at everyone.)* Shush! Now, everyone, listen!

(The lyrical sounds of Mendelsohn's 'A Midsummer Night's Dream' music steals through the theatre.)

BEATRICE: Ugh, God, not meddlesome Mendelsohn!

CHRISTABEL: *(In her own world.)* Yes…it's so seductively… and blissfully…magical, isn't it? *(Demonstrating.)* And I can just see David Rolls as Puck… When suddenly he swings into view on an invisible wire, and he lands…so fairy-like in a spotlight. *(Dancing towards MARK.)* Then he offers Oberon, the magic flower…like so! *(Giving an invisible flower to MARK.)* And the juice of the flower, you will squeeze…into my eyes, my Oberon, which, in turn, will make me – your Titania – fall into an enchanted sleep in the grove.

BILL: Yeah, but wot the 'Ell does Oberon want to do that for?

JO: He does it, Bill – because when Titania wakes up, she then instantly falls in love with - *you.*

BILL: Oh my Gawd!

MARTIN: But only after Puck has turned you into an ass, of course.

ROD: 'Cause it's your Bottom she's after.

BILL: Yeah, but that's nothing new because, round 'ere, I always 'ave to do all the donkey-work. Sorry. But I just couldn't resist it.

MARTIN: *(Flexing his muscles.)* Well…in days of yore, Reinhardt made his movie, using Mendelsohn, so I suppose I can play Oberon with the same salubrious soundtrack.

CHRISTABEL: Super! So give us a quick demo of your Oberon, Mark. Please. 'Cause you're bound to make him sound so sensuously sonorous.

MARTIN: Alright – if you absolutely insist.

BEATRICE: *(Frowning at her almost-empty glass of gin.)* Oh! Do you really have to?

MARTIN: *(Tossing a script to CHRISTABEL.)* You just stand there, baby, and read Puck's bits in between, OK?

CHRISTABEL: OK.

MARTIN: 'Ah, Puck, hast thou the flower there? Welcome, wanderer'…

BILL: *(Interrupting.)* 'Alf a mo! 'Alf a mo!

(BILL runs out into the audience, and goes into the lighting booth.)

JO: Where the hell are you off to?

BILL: If Mark's goin' to do 'is professional-nut, 'e needs the proper lightin', don't 'e?

JO: *(Shouting after him.)* But this isn't a performance, Bill!

ROD: It isn't even a goddamn rehearsal.

(Lights go down on the stage until there is only a spotlight, which MARTIN steps into.)

MARK: *(Speaking lyrically but resonantly against the music.)* Ah Puck, hast thou the flower there? Welcome, wanderer.

CHRISTABEL: *(Handing him a teaspoon.)* Ay, Master, here it is.

MARTIN: I pray thee, give it me.
I know a bank where the wild thyme blows,
Where oxlips and the nodding violent grows,
Quite over-canopied with luscious woodbine,
With sweet musk roses, and with eglantines.
There sleeps Titania sometimes of a night,
Lull'd with... *(JO turns the music off.)*
Why the hell did you do that?

CHRISTABEL: Yes, it was so lovely.

BEATRICE: True, it wasn't that bad, Joe. In fact Martin was speaking the verse tolerably well. For an actor.

MARTIN: Absolutely! So why did you switch it off?

JO: I'm sorry, Martin, but it was just too old fashioned.

(The lights come back up, and BILL returns to the stage.)

BILL: So wot's wrong wiv it bein' old-fashioned?

JO: Sorry, but they say that when Peter Brook did his radical production of *The Dream* for the RSC in 1970, *he* did it with *contemporary* Indian music, and he set it in a white gymnasium, with lots of juggling, and then apparently Puck swung in on a flying trapeze. And that was only Act One! So we, too, need to do something radically original.

BILLY: Yeah, but just then I had Mark lit to perfection!

JO: But that's not important, Bill. Like Brook did in his time, we also should be exploring the elements that are underlying Shakespeare's text; such as the Satanic sensuality which is bubbling away beneath *A Midsummer Night's Dream*.

ROD: Oh I see. Now I get it. You want Martin to play Oberon as a...well, as a sex-mad Dracula.

JO: No, Rod, of course, I don't. But instead of just indulging in all this bourgeois Middle Class lyricism, I want Martin to convey Oberon's...

MARTIN: *(Interrupting.)* ...Working Class Proletarian envy of Titania?

JO: No, I'm not suggesting that we do a Brechtian interpretation of *The Dream*.

MARTIN: No, but we could do a Freudian, or Jungian interpretation. Or even a Poor Theatre version of it.

BILL: Well, you can't get much poorer than us.

MARTIN: No, no, by Poor Theatre, I meant Theatre, with only the bare necessities, and without any frills.

ROD: You mean, like we normally do stuff.

(More weary laughter.)

MARTIN: Look, I'll show you what I mean. Now, Bill – give us a heart-beat on your drum.

BILL: *(Complying.)* Like this?

JO: Yes, Martin, but what's Bill drumming got to do with...?

BILL: *(Overriding her.)* Yeah, Martin, and wot about the lights? Oh, Rob, can you go and...?

MARTIN: *(Overriding him.)* No, we don't need the lights changed. We'll create the entire illusion with the Bard's words, and the audience's imagination.

BEATRICE: That'll be a first!

(MARTIN speaks the verse against the rhythm of the drum, and he brings out the sensual menace.)

MARTIN: 'There sleeps Titania, sometime of the night,
Lull'd in these flowers, with dances and delight,
And there the snake throws her enamell'd skin,
Weed wide enough to wrap a fairy in.
And with the juice of this, I streak her eyes,
And make her full of fearful fantasies'!

JO: Yes, that's the perfect blend of sadism and sensuality.

BILL: Well, I fink it's time for annuver cuppa.

JO: No, you should try to take this in, Bill, because Titania's relationship with your Bottom is to say the least marginally perverse.

CHRISTABEL: *(Giggling in delight.)* Really? I'd never noticed.

MARTIN: Well, don't you find it a bit kinky that a fairy should get the hots for a donkey. Even if he is well-hung.

BILL: Not if I'm the donging donkey, I don't.

BEATRICE: Quite right, William. You see, perversion is at the crux – and often at the crotch – of much of the world's mythology. Whether it be Leda having it off with a rampant swan. Or the aristocratic lady in *The Golden Ass* being mounted, and having riotous rumpy-pumpy with our four-footed friend here.

CHRISTABEL: Oh I didn't know that you had it in you, Beatrice.

MARTIN: Yes, because she doesn't, and hasn't. And that's half her problem.

BEATRICE: *(Tipsily upset.)* No, he's right, he's right! See, I don't mind a smattering of sex in literature. It's just the thought of it in *real* life…I mean, dear God!

JO: Everyone, shush, and let's get back to *The Dream*!

CHRISTABEL: No sooner said than done. So… *(Dancing around BEATRICE.)*
…'Newts and blind worms do no wrong;
And come not near our fairy queen.'

BEATRICE: I'm not your flipping fairy queen!

BILL: 'Course you are, baby. *(Now on the drums.)* So come on, you guys, let's have a jam session.

ROD: *(On his guitar.)* Yeah, go, man, go!

MARTIN: Yeah, let's really make it swing!

MARTIN starts to dance with CHRISTABEL, who continues singing.

BEATRICE: Are there no lower depths you won't plumb?

JO: You're right. *(In her best French accent.)* C'est quelle terrible!

The dancing figures of CHRISTABEL and MARK swirl around JO and BEATRICE.)

CHRISTABEL: 'Philomel with melody,
Sing in our sweet lullaby.
Lulla, lulla, lullaby, lulla, lullaby,
Never harm,
Nor spell, nor charm,
Come our lovely lady by;
So, good night, with lullaby.'

(Laughter and applause from BILL and ROD, and general falling about.)

JO: That was absolutely horrendous, not to mention *très horrifique*!

BEATRICE: So now you see what I mean, Jo. Immediately Shakespeare is brought to life, he is absolutely ruined. *(More laughter from the other four.)* No, what I really meant to say is, it's… *(Grabbing her empty glass.)* …well, it's time for another gin. And the barman had better go easy on the tossing tonic.

MARTIN: *(In his cod American accent)* And while you're at it, babes, as they ain't got no Guinness, go get me a quadruple scotch.

BEATRICE: *(Going.)* Typical. That's why all you actors are nothing but vacuous, idle, leeching and letching good-for-nothings!

MARTIN: *(Winking and maintaining his cod American accent.)* Thanks a bunch, doll-face. But don't forget the scotch.

(Still muttering to herself BEATRICE exits.)

ROD: Look, guys, can I say something?

JO: No, Rod! What I mean is… Well, can't it wait? 'Cause we've all got to go in a few minutes' time.

ROD: *(Nodding vigorously.)* And that's why I…

JO: *(Interrupting.)* Look, I know you're a very busy travel agent, Rod, and that you're kindly helping us out of a spot by giving us your Macduff, but…

ROD: *(Overriding her.)* That's what I wanna talk about.

JO: Yes, but we still haven't finished exploring *The Dream.*

ROD: Well, I'm sorry, Jo, but I just don't dig all this elf and goblin garbage. See, I'm used to working from a logical-intuitive, interior, psychological Freudian standpoint. And for the life of me, I don't find myself able to get inside the simpering psyche of a fagoty fairy!

MARTIN: Join the club, darling.

ROD: Of course *Macbeth* is a different can of worms entirely. 'Fact it's one helluva ballsy number. *(Pacing and waving his arms.)* I mean, Martin's such a lucky bastard.

MARTIN: Could've fooled me.

ROD: No, no, Martin, you're lucky as hell. 'Cause you're gonna play… *(Grabbing a sword out of the prop basket and waving it.)* …a poetic, psychopathic, Satanic, genocidal mass-murderer, who's perpetually freaked-out on a power-kick. I mean, Jesus, man, but that's just too much!

JO: You can say that again!

(JO flounces out.)

CHRISTABEL: She's got a weak bladder.

BILL: *(Waving a milk bottle.)* Same again for everyone?

MARTIN: *(Taking the sword from ROD and standing in the centre of the pentacle.).*
'And pity, like a new-born babe,
Striding the blast, or Heaven's cherubim horsed
Upon the sightless couriers of the air
Shall blow the horrid deed in every eye,
That tears shall drown the wind.'

(Pause.)

BILL: Blimey o'reily!

CHRISTABEL: *(Yawning and pencilling her eyebrows.)* Anything wrong, Billy?

BILL: No, but it's just a strange…painful way of puttin' it; 'Tears shall drown the wind.'

MARTIN: Oh I thought I was rather moving.

ROD: Don't you mean *Shakespeare* was rather moving?

MARTIN: Yes, you're right, Rod. *(Thrusting his sword back into the prop basket.)* Shakespeare's everything. While

we thespians are 'mere ciphers' to *his* 'great-accompt'.
Indeed, I often find the beauty of Shakespeare's language,
especially in *Macbeth* – well, it presents me as a 'mere
actor' with a lot of almost insoluble problems. I mean, for
a start, all that uplifting poetry seems to be totally at odds
with the psychological make-up of any mass-murderer in
history. And yet...and yet, as an actor, you've got to trust
Shakespeare's incredible language – because his language
gives you everything you need to enthral the audience.
*(CHRISTABEL yawns while she readjusts her décolletage, which
makes MARTIN explode.)* Oh for fuck's sake, stop thinking
about yourself for once, you yawning, preening bitch!

CHRISTABEL: Martin!

MARTIN: I'm sorry, Christabel, but everyone here is trying to
work out the best way of presenting Shakespeare, and all
you seem to do is yawn, play with your face, your hair,
your nails, and hitch up your fornicating bra.

CHRISTABEL: I'm sorry, but the reason I...

MARTIN: *(Overriding her.)* Look, I don't mean to hurt you,
sweetheart, but what I'm getting at is this; I came down
here to try and be of some help to you all. But I can't
do that unless you're prepared to steep yourselves in
Shakespeare's words, because that's where he's hidden all
the dramatic dimensions of your parts, and of his plays.

CHRISTABEL: Yes, but what...

JO returns, and interrupts her.

JO: No, no, he's right, Chrissy. And it's what I've been saying
all along.

CHRISTABEL: *(Flouncing around the stage.)* Yes, but now I want
to talk about *me,* and my acting problems!

MARTIN: Oh this is totally hopeless. *(Snatching the sword from
the prop basket.)* So let's forget truth, subtlety, and above all,
let's trample and traduce beauty. Yes, and instead, we'll

do it like Henry Irving and Donald Wolfit did it in the old days, with the full-blown *sturm und drang*! *(Now waving his sword and bellowing.)*

So…'Hang out our banners on the outward walls;
The cry is still, 'They come. So arm, arm and out!''

BILL: *(Rushing off the stage.)* You bet ya!

MARTIN: 'I 'gin to grow aweary of the sun,
And I wish the state o' the world were now undone.
Ring the alarum bell!'

(As if on cue, BILL re-appears, frenziedly beating a gong.)

BILL: *(About his gong.)* This is better than a bell, 'cause it's a helluva lot louder! *(By now ROD has grabbed a trumpet, and he is blowing it for all its worth.)* Oh Rob, that's better'n better. 'Cause when fings are getting' borin', you can't beat a bit of noise.

MARTIN: 'So blow, wind! come, wrack!
At least we'll die with harness on our back!'

(MARTIN discards his sword. Then he crosses to the laughing TRUMPETER and the equally-laughing GONG-BEATER, and MARTIN accompanies them by doing his own frenzied war-beat on the drum. Combined with the TRIO's continuous laughter, the total din is discordant and ear-splitting. So much so, the much-discomforted CHRISTABEL and JO have their ears covered.)

CHRISTABEL: *(Shouting.)* Stop it, the three of you, stop it! You're going to burst my delicate eardrums!

JO: *(Also with her hands over her ears.)* Yes, you sadistic sods, you've more than made your piss-poor points! *(Still laughing the TRIO eventually relents. Then their horrendous din subsides. Shaking her head in disbelief, JO removes her hands from her ears.)* Well, all I can say is thank God for small mercies. *(Then she crosses to BILL.)* Now the least you can do, Bill, is give me a spare fag. Please!

BILL: Can't. Sorry.

JO: Why not?

BILL: I've given smoking' for Lent. *(Pulling his chewing gum out of his mouth.)* That's why I'm always chewin' this crap.

JO: Oh God, this is just like a big peep into Purgatory!

CHRISTABEL: *(Tearfully.)* Yes! 'Cause no one ever wants to talk about *me*! Oh, I know I'm a bit scatty, and I often look completely out of it… *(Pointing to her forehead.)* … but there is a helluva lot going on inside here. I mean, do you realise that you've all been wittering on and on about Shakespeare's Scottish answer to… *(Pointing at MARTIN.)* … well, to Sean Connery over there. But none of you have made one single mention about *me* as Lady Macbeth. Except to refer to me as a yawning, bra-hitching, bitch of a bimbo!

ROD: Yeah, Jo, and while we're on the subject of *Macbeth*, I think we should cut the Porter Scene entirely.

CHRISTABEL: I'm not talking about the frigging Porter Scene, I'm talking about…

JO: *(Overriding her, to ROD.)* There's no way we're going to cut the Porter Scene. But, anyway, thanks for reminding me. *(To BILL.)* Because I meant to tell you, Bill, that as well as you giving us your Bottom, you're also going to give us your alcoholic Porter.

BILL: Oh shit a brick!

ROD: That's why I say the Porter should be cut, Jo. I mean, how could Shakespeare dream of bringing in such a drunken bum into the middle of his otherwise-sublime tragedy?

MARTIN: The reason is simple, Rob – because, as the great Laurence Olivier would have said – had he thought of it… *(Doing his Olivier imitation.)* …After the murder of King Duncan, The Bard brings in the drunken Porter, in order to break the tension at that critical point in his drama. Just like *I'm* doing now, laddie.

ROD: Yeah, but I still say… *(He trails off as his hands cover his crotch.)* Oh screwing scrotums! My zip's gone again!

MARTIN: *(In his John Gielgud accent.)* Oh don't worry, we can still use you, Rodney. See, Shakespeare always wrote the odd role for a numbskull, navel clown.

ROD: *(Rummaging in the tool bag.)* Where the hell did I put those pissing pliers?

CHRISTABEL: *(Who by now has slumped onto a chair, and she is dabbing her tears.)* No question about it. I'm just like Masha in *The Seagull* because 'I am…in mourning for my life'.

BILL: *(Banging the drum and singing.)*
'The woosell cock so black of hue,
With orange tawny bill…

JO: Bill, please, don't make things even worse!

(BILL stops drumming, but he continues to sing as he moves towards the tearful CHRISTABEL.)

BILL: 'The throstle with his note so true,
The wren with his little quill…'

(As he sings, he kneels on the stage, and puts his head into CHRISTABEL's lap.)

CHRISTABEL: Hey, where the hell d'you think you're putting your head, Bill?

BILL: No, accordin' to Old Shakebag – as Queen Tits-tania – you should reply; 'Wot angel wakes me from my flowery bed?'

CHRISTABEL: Bill, get off me! Jo, get him off me! Well, you're supposed to be the director, so direct him!

JO: *(Picking MARTIN's newspaper and reading it.)* Too late, Tits-tania. See, I've given up.

MARTIN: *(Snatching his newspaper off her.)* What?

JO: No, I mean it. *(Enter BEATRICE, with her gin and MARTIN's scotch, and she is now very drunk.)* You can all do exactly as you like.

Snorting MARTIN sits and reads his newspaper.

MARTIN: Right, but I'm not leaving 'till you give me the sub you promised me.

JO: Fine. *(Sitting and drinking her tea.)* See, I don't give a tinker's toss.

BEATRICE: Good. 'Cause now things are bound to improve.

BILL: Well, you lot may not wanna rehearse, but I'm still gonna give me bleedin' Bottom, 'cause soon it'll be closin' time!
Marching around the stage drumming and singing.
'The finch, the sparrow and the lark,
the plainsong cuckoo grey...'

BEATRICE: *(Slurring her words and nodding.)*
Yes...'Life's but a walking shadow, a poor player,
That struts and frets his hour upon the stage.'

BILL: *(Overlapping her with his singing.)*
'Whose note full many a man doth mark,
And does not say him nay!'
(Speaking.) But now I need to go for a piss...
So all I can say...
...is 'Hip-hip Pissin' Hooray'!

(BILL exits running as CHRISTABEL shakes off her tears, and goes into her sexy-fairy-song-and-dance-routine.)

CHRISTABEL: 'So let every fairy take his gait,
And every several chamber bless,
Through this palace with sweet peace...'

ROD: *(Holding onto his zipper.)* Oh this stupendous! *(Picking up his sword and moving behind the seated MARTIN.)* 'Macbeth! Turn, hell-hound, turn!'

CHRISTABEL: *(Now her giggling self again.)* Oh, Rod, you do look so sweet holding onto your rod and your grapes!

(MARTIN discards his newspaper, grabs a sword, and then he confronts ROD.)

MARTIN: 'Macduff, of all men, I have avoided thee.
But get thee back…
(Laughing and pointing his sword at ROD's crotch.)
…my soul is too much charged
With blood of thine already!'

ROD: *(Still struggling unsuccessfully with his zipper.)*
'I have no words.
My voice is in…
(Laughing as he indicates his groin.) …my sword.'

MARTIN: *(Now finding it difficult to speak because he's laughing so much.)* 'Well, lay on, Macduff,
And damn'd be him who first cries; "Hold! Enough!"'

Still laughing hysterically ROD and MARTIN start fighting laboriously and incompetently.

BEATRICE: *(Waving her arms in disgust.)* If you're all going to spoil things by actually rehearsing, then I'm going to hit the bar again!

CHRISTABEL: I don't understand why you bothered to join our Society in the first place.

BEATRICE: I would have thought that was obvious. I joined 'cause… *(Picking up her glass.)* …you have a very cute barman.

BEATRICE staggers off towards the bar while MARTIN and ROD continue to laugh and fight.

CHRISTABEL: Hey, you guys, watch where you're swinging those slashing swords!

ROD: Yeah, steady, man, steady on! 'Cause I'm supposed to win this!

CHRISTABEL: *(Laughing as she puts the Mendelsohn CD on again, and then she sings and dances to it.)*
'If we shadows have offended,
Think but this, and all is mended!
That you have but slumbered here
While these visions did appear.'

ROD: *(Stabbing MARTIN under the arm)* You're dead now, you're dead! Well, fall over for, Chrissakes!

MARTIN: Oh, sure. For a moment, I forgot. *(Falling over and doing an Olivier-type death.)* 'My kingdom…for a horse!'

CHRISTABEL: 'So goodnight unto you all.'

ROD: *(Kneeling at the feet of JO, who is still sitting and scowling.)*
'Hail, King Malcolm! For so thou art. Behold where stands
The usurper's cursed head!'

CHRISTABEL: *(Helping MARTIN to his feet.)*
'So give me your hands, if we be friends,
And Robin shall restore amends.'

JO: *(Giving them all a derisive slow hand-clap.)* Right, children, right! *(Pushing out the Mendelsohn CD.)* That's more than a godawful-enough for tonight. Class dismissed! You're all dismissed!

(She is about to storm out when CHRISTABEL pulls her back.)

CHRISTABEL: Oh, you're going to go off in one of your schoolmistress' huffs, are you?

JO: Now don't you bring my classroom problems into this! *(Near to tears.)* I have more than enough of them during the week, without...! So goodnight, goodnight, everyone. *(As BILL re-enters.)* Thank God, tomorrow is another day.

BILL: But wot about our rehearsal?

JO: *(Erupting.)* What rehearsal, you boorish bumholes? 'Cause you're nothing but rotten, perverse, uneducated bastards! And bitches!

BILL: Oh, now even *she's* cracked! What a total shoggin' shambles.

JO: *(To them all.)* Can't you see that you've ruined and destroyed everything?

MARTIN: *(Putting his arm around her.)* That's nonsense, Jo. It was just an excess of high spirits, that's all.

JO: *(Moving away from him.)* Yes, but you made fun of Shakespeare. And there is no greater crime under the sun. It's sacrilege. Because you have all deliberately sabotaged the Bard of Avon. And, what's more, you've done it on his bloody birthday!

MARTIN: *(Smiling and shaking his head.)* Impossible, love. Shakespeare is so fantastic, he can survive anything. Even us.

JO: But I wanted my productions to be different, and to have that...well, that *je ne sais quoi.*

MARTIN: Well, they're certainly going to have that.

ROD: Yeah, and it's all been a lot of fun. And the fight mended my zip.

JO: You horrible, unfeeling animals! Well, can't you see how ludicrous and embarrassing you've all been?

CHRISTABEL: No, Jo. We made a...well, we made a kinda magic just then...

JO: Magic?!

MARTIN: *(In his cod American.)* Yeah, we created a cool collage with wondrous sounds and action.

JO: I simply don't believe I'm part of this crapulous anarchic shambles.

BILL: Look, don't get your panties in a twist, Jo. See even when we're doin' dumb fings wiv 'is words, Old Shakebag's still 'avin' the last larf. No, really. While we're poncin' around like wallies, and makin' right tits of ourselves, Old Shakebag's hoverin' above us, wiv 'is birthday tankard of porter, and he's pissin' 'imself wiv laughter.

JO: No, no, it's awful what we've done. Just awful!

MARTIN: Oh do stop fretting, Joe. By the time we've thrown these plays on the stage, whatever their chaotic condition, at least we will all have learnt something. And learning is everything. *(Putting his arm around JO's shoulder.)* Now come on, Josephine, let Emperor Napoleon buy you a drinkie-pooh or two.

(The now-very-drunk BEATRICE staggers in.)

BEATRICE: Too late. The fucking bar's closed!

JO: But I must have a drink!

BEATRICE: *(Slurring her words.)* But as it's old Willy Shakebag's birthday, you can all come back to my place for…several night-caps, and then we can drink the Old Bugger's health.

CHRISTABEL: *(Singing and dancing round them.)*
'A great while ago, and the world began,
With heigh, ho, the wind and the rain…'

ROD: Must say, I'm glad I'm only a visitor.

CHRISTABEL/MARTIN: *(Now singing together as they exit hand-in-hand.)* 'And that's all one, our play is done,
And we'll strive to please you everyday.'

LIGHTS fade.

The End.

SUCCUBUS
A PLAY IN ONE ACT

Characters

LILI

MARK HOPKINS

The basement in MARK HOPKINS' Victorian house. Rimpton Village. Cornwall.

Time; the Present. Lammas Night. (First of August.)

MARK's basement is shrouded in shadows, but we can just make out the black curtain that covers the door, behind which are the stairs leading up to the ground floor.

Footsteps are heard echoing down the basement steps.

Moments later, the basement door creaks open behind the black curtain. Then the curtain is drawn back.

A WOMAN, in a figure-revealing dress, comes into the basement, closing the curtain behind her. She is carrying a floppy bag over her shoulder, but the shadows shroud her features.

The WOMAN crosses the basement, and approaches what we realise is a table. Then she lights two tall candles in ornate candlesticks on the table.

The candlelight illuminates the white lace cloth that covers the table, and also the rest of the basement, which now looks somewhat like an austere chapel. In front of the table, on a grey rug, there are four upright chairs facing the altar-like table. At odds with the chapel-image, there is a tall free-standing bookshelf, which is filled with antique tomes.

The WOMAN puts down her floppy bag on a chair. Then she moves behind the altar-like-table. For the first time we see her clearly. She is in her late thirties, with long hair on her shoulders. She is both seductive and mischievous, but at times there is a profound sadness about her.

She lifts up the hem of the tablecloth, and she is foraging under the table, when she hears footsteps echoing down the basement steps.

Smiling the WOMAN adjusts the tablecloth. Then she moves away from the table. She sits in one of the chairs, with her back to us...as the basement door creaks open.

A bearded MAN, in his early forties, who is physically very fit, swishes back the curtain covering the door. Then he surges into the basement.

In fuming disbelief he registers the presence of the unconcerned, seated WOMAN, and the flickering candles behind her.

In response the bearded MAN wrenches the curtain back over the basement door. Then he advances on the seated WOMAN, who remains motionless. The MAN has an American accent.

MAN: What the hell d'you think you're doing?

WOMAN: *(Still with her back to him.)* I'm enjoying the view.

The MAN points to the candlelit table.

MAN: That's not a view! It's the…the…

The MAN trails off as the WOMAN turns her chair towards him, with a beneficent smile.

WOMAN: I know exactly what it is.

Furiously the MAN scratches his beard, gesturing at the white-clothed table.

MAN: What right have you to pry in here?

WOMAN: You said come round, remember?

MAN: Yeah, but I didn't say you could mosey down into my basement!

The WOMAN shakes her head as she watches the MAN continue to scratch his beard frenziedly.

WOMAN: Beards and excema don't make good bed-fellows, Mark. Shave it off before you scratch yourself to death.

In response MARK starts to jog up and down on the spot.

MARK: You're trouble, Lili. Y'know that? You're real trouble.

LILI: Yes, but if you weren't seriously suffering, Mark, you wouldn't have asked me round so late, would you? And by the way you're jigging and jogging, we're not talking just excema here.

Momentarily MARK stops jogging.

MARK: If you've come to help me, why the hell are you just sitting there like the proverbial Sphinx?

LILI: *(Smiling.)* In that regard – you may be much nearer the 'Mark' than you think.

MARK: That's a dreadfully-horrendous pun.

LILI: You should know. You're the writer.

He moves to the curtained door.

MARK: Let's go upstairs.

LILI: We'll do it here.

MARK: No!

LILI: *(Amused.)* You worried we'll be discovered?

(MARK indicates the candlelit table.)

MARK: No, it's just… *(He trails off, and starts jogging again.)* Anyway, *you're* the one who should be worrying, Lili.

LILI: Really. *(She points at him jogging.)* When it's *you* who's about to detonate.

MARK: OK, OK. *(He continues to jog.)* We can…do it here. *(Uncertainly.)* And then hopefully I'll…be forgiven.

LILI rises from her chair.

LILI: So stop bobbing up and down like a puppet on a chain, and sit here. *(She points to her chair.)* Then we can begin.

MARK shakes his head vehemently and goes on jogging.

MARK: I can't sit there with my back to…

LILI: …Your altar?

MARK: It's not mine!

LILI: As you will. *(LILI moves her chair away from the altar.)* Sit over here, then. Where you might find it to be marginally less profane.

MARK is now jumping up and down on the spot.

MARK: You'll pay for this!

LILI: *(Amused.)* No, *you're* the one who's paying.

MARK: *(As he jumps up and down on the spot.)* True. But, let me tell you…I know a darn sight more…about you…than you think.

LILI: Do you now?

MARK: You bet ya.

LILI watches him continue to jump up and down on the spot.

LILI: But the question remains, Mister Fitness Freak…do you want me to ease your very obvious distress? Or don't you?

MARK: Yeah, I do. *(Momentarily he stops jumping.)* What's more, Lili baby, I'm glad you've shimmied down into my basement.

LILI: Good.

MARK: But *you* may not be so enthusiastic before we're done.

He starts jogging again.

LILI: I've always taken all my chances, Mark. *(She points to the chair.)* So – before you have a heart-attack, you'd best give Puffing Billy a rest, and park your bobbing butt here, like a gut kleine mensch. Then I will bring you the relief you so desperately crave.

MARK: I thought you'd be the first to understand… *(He points to his jogging feet.)* …that I can't stop doing this because…

LILI: *(Overriding him.)* Yes, but if *you* don't stop dancing in front of the Lord Thy God, and sit down, then, in your recently-acquired Yankee Doodle parlance… *(In a cod American accent.)* … 'I'm going to do nuthin' for you, Mark baby, 'cause I'm outta here pronto!'

MARK stops jogging.

MARK: No, no, please don't go, Lili! And I'll do just as you say. *(Reluctantly he sits in the chair.)* Truth is… *(He points to the flickering candles.)* …there are many ways to honour Him, but my way is to try to keep myself fit for His Purpose. *(He gazes balefully at her.)* 'Cause He told me, see, that – in *your* case, Lili – the end truly justifies whatever the means.

LILI: *(Laughing.)* Since when has Karl Marx been your other pillow companion?

MARK springs out of his chair, inadvertently knocking it over.

MARK: Is nothing sacred to you, Lili? With your crass Bolshi jokes.

LILI returns the chair to its standing position.

LILI: More to the point, Mark, when you were on your nocturnal-run through the countryside tonight, suddenly you found yourself standing in the bluebell glade in Hangland's Wood, didn't you?

MARK: *(Disconcerted.)* How the devil d'you know that?

LILI: Most folk, with a semblance of imagination, find themselves enthralled by the beatific vision of the rising August moon.

MARK: Yeah, and especially when it's full and brazen - like *you* are!

LILI: *(Smiling.)* Of course. That's often how you think of me, isn't it?

Feverishly MARK clutches his forehead.

MARK: Oh, for mercy's sake, Lili, can't you just bring me some relief?

LILI: Then cease hyperventilating, sit down again, and try to relax. And I will relieve you…of yourself.

Reluctantly MARK sits in the chair.

MARK: I should never have come to see you in the first place.

LILI: That's what they all say.

But to whomever they pray,
Still every man jack,
They always keeps coming back.

MARK: *(Shaking his head vehemently.)* It's so wrong that someone like you should possess the gifts you have.

LILI: Every gift comes at a price.

MARK: Yeah, but you haven't paid the price for any of your 'gifts' yet, have you, Lili?

LILI: *(Momentarily desolate.)* Many more times than you can possibly conceive. Now…try to empty your mind.

Frenziedly he clutches his forehead.

MARK: How can I? When I'm on fire in here!

LILI: I know you are. But your only hope for solace is to place your hands on your thighs, and then – you must try to empty your mind.

He obeys her.

MARK: I'm trying, God help me, I'm trying! But it's like…an inferno in here!… And everywhere!

LILI moves behind him, and places her hands either side of his head, but she still does not touch him.

LILI: Of course it is. And your particular torment will always consume you, Mark, until you exorcise all your demons.

MARK: Hm! Demons are *your* province, baby, not mine. *You're* the goddam succubus!

LILI: It takes an incubus to know one.

MARK: Oh stop torturing me, woman, and, for God's sake, do what you do!

LILI: Before I touch you, and do what you want me to do to you; first you have to close your eyes. Then you must imagine that you have stopped running in Hangland's

Wood. And now you are standing in the sacred bluebell glade where - once again – you are being bathed in the restorative rays...of the seraphic Moon.

In response MARK stands abruptly. Then he moves away from her.

MARK: Look, there's no way I can do it here! It's ...it's...well, it's sacrilegious. So let's go do it upstairs.

LILI: We'll do it here, or nowhere, Mark. Or I won't touch you. Anywhere. And if I *don't* touch you – then, like last night – you will burn in purgatory 'till daybreak. And you'll still have to run over to my cottage first thing tomorrow morning, where you will beg me to bring you the same relief.

MARK: Yeah, yeah, you're right, God damn you! Despite everything I try to do – or be – for Him, my only reward is this relentless... *(Fiercely he massages his cranium.)* ...inferno in here.

LILI: Then stop fighting me, and obey me, 'Saint' Mark.

MARK: OK, OK. But enough of the blasphemous jokes.

LILI: So obey me, and sit down.

MARK: *(Sitting down again.)* As you will.

LILI: No, as *She* wills. *(She moves behind him.)* Close your eyes. *(He obeys her.)* And, once again, submerge yourself in the ever-healing light...of the full moon at Lammas-tide. *(Her hands transcribe an invisible halo around his head.)* So... now...have you con-jured up Her Omnipresent, Iridescent Sphere...in your mind's eye?

MARK: Heaven help me, I'm doing my best, but I'm still burning. See, what you're asking me to do, well, it goes against absolutely everything I believe in. But I'll try anything...for a moment's peace. Yeah...yeah... *(With his eyes closed, he nods his head.)* ...yes, now I'm...once again...a shadow in among the dead bluebells... And I'm...yes, I'm floating in a sea of...moonlight. So, please...I beg you...

129

just get on with it…and bring me some relief. *(LILI begins to massage his cranium.)* Oh sweet Jesus, you only have to touch me, Lili, and your fingers are like…well, they're like the foam on the moon-washed ocean…and almost instantly all the flames and the horrific heat…recedes… And you do it as if by…

LILI: *(Smiling.)* …An occult, lunar conjuration?

MARK: Yeah… And now if only you'd… if you'd please… please…just…just…

Still with his eyes closed, MARK trails off and shakes his head.

LILI: Ask…and you may well receive.

LILI's fingers are now massaging MARK's neck.

MARK: Lower…stroke me…with those enticing fingers… lower, Lili…lower… *(In response LILI's fingers caress his chest.)* Now even lower!

LILI: First you must confess to Her…the enormity of all that you have done *against* Her. Or you will continue to suffer this burning anguish from here to eternity.

MARK: Lower, you bitch, stroke me lower. No, no, much, much lower still!

LILI: So what price is *his* help now, Mr Hopkins?

MARK: Yes, The Lord God said that you are even worse than the Whore of Babylon! And, Christ help me, He is right!

MARK surges to his feet, knocking his chair over. Then he grabs LILI, and savagely kisses her. But after a brief struggle, LILI manages to break away from him.

LILI: *He* didn't call me 'The Whore of Babylon'. They are *your* words, Mark, not his. But as I keep telling you, the only way you will ever break out of the torture chamber that's incinerating your mind, is if you summon up the courage to confront your deviant image in the mirror. Then you must confess all your innumerable sins to Her!

MARK: No, it's *you*, you succubus, who should confess that every night you come to me in my dreams, but you never let me possess you. So if there is a 'godless deviant', then sure as there is Hell; it's *you*!

LILI: That's what I mean. You only want to 'possess', not to 'love'. But then you never talk about 'love', do you, Mark?

MARK: You're spouting garbage! I love and worship *Him*! That's more than enough 'love' for any man. And it should be enough for any goddamn woman, too! *(He plucks a paperback from the bookshelf and waves it at her.)* That's what I've written about in here! I'm one of the few modern children's story-writers that teaches the kids about the importance of the love of God. See, those poor little creatures need some Christian values, to help 'em in this cesspit of a world!

LILI: But who created 'this cesspit of a world'?

MARK: Us humans! The Lord God gave us Free Will, and *this* is what we did with *His* World!

LILI: There was – and always is – another Way, Mark. Yet since your childhood – like so many others before you – you have deviated from the Way and the Light of the Moon.

MARK: You know nothing about my childhood.

LILI: I know that your mother left you when you needed her most. Not that she had much choice in the matter, of course.

MARK: *(Shaking his head in disbelief.)* Next you'll be saying you can read my frigging mind!

LILI: Give me your hands.

MARK: What?

LILI: Both hands.

MARK: Why?

LILI: You know you want to.

MARK: Why'd you want my hands?

LILI: It's in your eyes.

MARK: What? My hands?

LILI: No, the pain. And the pain has been there, ever since your mother died when you were only a teenager.

MARK: You can see that…in my eyes?

LILI: Yes.

MARK: God in Heaven.

LILI: That's debatable. But to this day, you can never forget that night when you were only seven-years-old, can you? You were so terrified that the moon was coming through the window to possess you that your mother had to stroke your hands and your face for over two hours, 'till your fear passed. And since your mother died, amongst all the other things that haunt you, deep inside you, there has always been this maternal abyss. That's why you must confront your fear now. So do as I say; and give me your hands.

MARK: It's not my hands that need stroking.

LILI: *(Shaking her head.)* Love, not desire, Mark. Love is the only certain way that you will ever find salvation.

MARK: Oh right on! *(Laughing.)* You want me to love your sodding moon, don't you? I know that's *your* creed, Lili. And in the moon's name, you've done the most terrible things.

LILI: Oh, surely you don't believe everything you've read, do you?

MARK: Yeah, I do. That's why you've got to be stopped. And it's why I'm glad that you've invaded my sanctuary voluntarily.

LILI: Look, I only came here to try and save you from yourself. But it seems that's not what you want… *(She picks up her floppy bag from the chair.)* …so I think it's time I went.

MARK: No, it's my turn now, baby!

LILI: Are you forcibly going to try to prevent me from leaving? Like the others did.

MARK: You bet ya. See, like it or not, baby, you're staying down here in my basement with me, 'till I'm done with you.

MARK pulls back the curtain covering the basement door. In response LILI crosses towards him, but MARK ignores her and locks the door. Then he pockets the key.

LILI: OK, you've had your fun, Mark. So unlock the door.

MARK: No way. See, I'm doing His Will.

LILI: *(Laughing.)* And 'Do What Thou Wilt shall be the Whole of the Law', right?

MARK: No. That's the Satanic dictum of that bogus warlock, Aleister Crowley. And it's what *you* believe, isn't it?

LILI: I certainly don't believe – as Aleister Crowley did – that 'The Prince of Darkness is a gentleman'. Anymore than *you* are proving to be a gentleman.

MARK: Yeah, but more to the point, Lili. What about the *other* 'gentlemen' in your recent life?

LILI: What about them?

MARK: You've had two guys in barely two years. 'Fact more like two in eighteen months. And God knows how many others before them.

LILI: Yes, but the world is a vast place, and I find staying two years anywhere can often seem like an eternity.

MARK: So why'd you come here two years ago?

She takes some lipstick from her bag, and applies it to her lips.

LILI: Because I had – and still have – some unfinished business in this village.

MARK: You've done enough damage around here. What the hell else have you got in mind?

LILI: In the hole where your heart should be, Mark, you already know the answer to that.

MARK: You're not making sense. 'Specially as you've been sleeping alone for over half a year now, and that's not your style. Well, your bed's been empty these last six months, hasn't it?

LILI: Has it?

MARK: Yeah. See, I've been watching you.

LILI: And that's one of the many reasons that *you* can't sleep at all, isn't it, Emperor All-Seeing-Marcus Aurelius?

MARK: Playing these asinine games with my name's not gonna help you. 'Cause there's no way you can shrug off the awful things you did to your last two gents. *(LILI pulls a half-full wine bottle out of her floppy bag. Then she removes the screw-top, and takes a sip from her wine bottle.)* You can't drink in here!

LILI: Yes, and talking of 'gents' – now that you have incarcerated me here – if *you* were one, then, at the very least, you would have offered me a much-appreciated glass of chilled vino. But as you're not a gent, you didn't, so…

MARK: So I don't drink! OK? Well, not since…

He trails off.

LILI: *(Finishing his thought.)* …You faced up to being an alcoholic in the U.S. of A.

MARK: Who told you…?

LILI: *(Overriding him.)* Or why else did you go straight into rehab when you got back from the Mid West? And then within weeks of coming out of rehab, you became a… *(In her cod American accent.)* …a keep-fit-fanatic, jig-jogging, Born-Again Christian?

MARK: Jesus Christ!

LILI: Yes, that – I understand – *is* his name. So I rest my post-alchi-keep-fit-jogging-Born-Again-Christian-case. *(After taking another sip of wine.)* And, indeed, as a result, you now only sip Ribena when you take Communion.

MARK: *You're* a one to talk. With the shitty things you do.

LILI: Such as?

MARK: Stop playing the innocent. See, while you were out of your cottage last week, I went into your bedroom.

LILI: *(Returning the wine bottle to her floppy bag.)* I know.

MARK: And there's not a single photo of you in there. 'Fact there are no photos of you in your cottage anywhere. Not even with any of your lovers.

LILI: How many lovers did you have in mind? *(She rummages in her floppy bag, and pulls out a bag of cherries.)* Savour one or two of my cherries. They might sweeten you up.

MARK: I don't *eat* in here, either.

LILI: *(After savouring a cherry.)* Surely you have the odd sanctified wafer?

MARK: Are there no depths you won't plumb?

LILI: *(Putting the bag of cherries on an adjacent chair.)* You're imprisoning *me*, remember. Not visa versa. And I am feeling rather peckish for something delectably-juicy.

MARK: Truth is, you're scared shitless of being photographed, aren't you?

LILI: *(Amused as she enjoys her cherries.)* You think I'm some kind of vampire, then?

MARK: You're not just a congenital cherry-sucker.

LILI: Charmed, I'm sure.

MARK: But don't you worry your pretty little fangs. I've still got you sorted as far as a photo of you is concerned. And I've taken a real beauty of you, baby. So d'you wanna see your latest mugshot? *(In response LILI puts three of the four chairs together, so that the chairs resemble a wooden bench.)* What you playing at now?

LILI reclines on the three chairs as if it was a chaiselongue.

LILI: I'm making myself comfortable for the interrogation.

MARK: Good. 'Cause when I couldn't sleep last night, I ran over to your cottage, and I took a snapshot of you through your open window. *(He points at LILI, who is reclining on the chairs.)* Yeah, Sweet Lips, and you were lying on your chaiselongue in the moonlight – very much like you're doing now – only last night you didn't have any clothes on. And that's how I like you. So are you ready to be knocked out by my risque portrait of you?

LILI: This is your torture chamber, and you, Mark, are Torquemada. So what choice have I, but to supinely acquiesce to your every desire? Though, I must warn you, very little will come of it. But if it will give you a frisson; why don't you take it out of your wallet and show me?

MARK: How'd you know it's in my…?

LILI: *(Overriding him and pointing to his pocket.)* You haven't got a girlfriend, so I'm certain that I'm all alone in there - rubbing against your upper groin.

MARK: This is what you did to the other two, isn't it?

LILI: Would you like me to put my hand in your pocket and see if I can…find it?

MARK: *(Shaking his head vigorously.)* Yeah.

LILI: And when I've got hold of it, you'd like me to...pull it out, wouldn't you?

MARK: *(Continuing to shake his head vigorously.)* Yes, oh yes, baby...

LILI: Then come here...like a good little boy.

MARK: *(Coming close to her.)* I'm not 'little'!

LILI: That's what they all say.

MARK: *(Moving back from her.)* I'm sick of your mind-games!

LILI: It's you men who have invented all the games. We women prefer reality.

MARK: Then here's reality for you! *(He pulls his wallet out of his pocket.)* Now you'll see how stark-bollock naked you are!

LILI: *(Laughing)* I think testicles are more your province.

MARK hurls his wallet at her, which she catches adroitly.

MARK: God, the things I'm gonna do to you! They don't bear thinking about!

LILI: Then don't think about them. But, of course, one of your many problems is you're rotting away with loneliness.

MARK snatches the wallet out of her hand.

MARK: No, it's *you*, who is the seriously sick bitch, so you're the one who is about to face yourself. *(He pulls a snapshot out of his wallet.)* Now take a long look-see at *that!* 'Cause that is you – totally *in love* with *you*, baby!

He waves the snapshot in her face.

LILI: *(Smiling serenely.)* Perfection, isn't it? As divinely-white and chaste as the fully-risen Lammas moon.

MARK: There's nothing 'chaste' about it! It was a fucking succubus I photographed.

LILI: If you look at it again, you'll see that I'm right.

MARK looks at the snapshot, and he is dumbfounded by what he sees.

MARK: This is… utterly impossible!

LILI: Isn't it just? So describe what you see – baby.

MARK: All I can see is…the moon. It's just a snapshot of the full-frigging-moon. But I pointed my camera at *you* through your goddam window, Lili, and you were absolutely starkers! And you were…you were…

LILI: *(Shaking her head.)* No, that's just how you *imagined* me to be, because it's how you *wanted* me to be. But, you see, the Goddess would have none of it, so She insisted that you take a photograph of *Her* Reflection in my window.

MARK: But I was there, and *you* were lying on your godamn sofa, and you were totally nude, and you were playing with your…

LILI: *(Overriding him.)* No, no, Mark. It was your licentious mind that was 'playing' testosterone tricks on you again, in yet another of your sleepless dreams.

MARK: Yeah, yeah, of course! You did the same to those other guys, didn't you? With your body and your mind-games, you went on teasing poor Brackenbury 'till the dumb dickhead couldn't take anymore.

LILI: It takes a dumb dickhead to know one.

MARK: I'm talking about what happened to Brackenbury!

LILI: And I'm telling you, 'boyo', that nothing is ever as it seems. Like your imagined snapshot of me.

MARK: Listen, there's no way you can get out of what you did to Brackenbury. Yeah, I know Tom was weak, but he was still a helluva good guy.

LILI savours another cherry.

LILI: You talk as if he's passed away, when he's still very much with us.

MARK: Yeah, but Tom's been sectioned 'cause of *you*. So now the poor bastard's stuck for God knows how long in the Lea.

LILI: *(Eating another cherry.)* Like *you*, Mark, Brackenbury was physically stronger than me. But most men are. Though most men don't attack me. At least not like *you* attacked me just now. And Brackenbury was even more violent than you. Mind, in *his* case, it wasn't the first time that he'd attacked me, either. And, indeed, on the night in question, your 'weak but helluva good guy' went on and on attacking me relentlessly.

MARK: 'Course, he went for you. You're enough to drive any guy nuts! *(He slumps into a chair.)* What's worse, I bet you don't ever visit Tom in the Lea, to see how the poor sod's getting on, do you?

LILI: *(Returning her cherries into her floppy bag.)* You're the one who's always tailing me, so you tell me.

MARK: Darn right I tail you. Someone's gotta catch you out, and make you pay for the godawful things you've done. See, you're the only reason that Tom's incarcerated in a nuthouse, where he's drooling like a toothless baba.

LILI stands, and holds out her hand.

LILI: Then hadn't you best give me the key to my prison, Mark, before the same thing happens to you?

MARK: What you did to Tom is not you at your worst, though, is it?

LILI: Just give me the key, Mark, and we'll call it a night.

MARK: No way. See, nothing about you makes any sense. For starters, when they found Bobby Heron in the wood next to your cottage, why didn't the cops arrest you?

LILI: Why should they? When everyone – but you – agrees that Bobby did it quite willingly. So now stop filibustering, Mark, and open this dungeon like a good little boy.

MARK: How many times do I have to tell you? It's not 'little', you vicious cow. I've got a whopper in here! *(He raises his hand to hit her, but she just smiles at him. Shaking his head he lowers his hand.)* Yeah, 'course. You indulge in these sexually-humiliating games because they're all part of your succubus bag of tricks, aren't they?

LILI: Then you'd best be careful what you lust after, mister, or you may get an infinitely greater climax than you've bargained for.

MARK: You're a bottomless pit of filth, aren't you?

LILI moves around him provocatively.

LILI: You're the one who's aching for it, and who's constantly ogling my every contour.

MARK: Look, you can't duck out of it like that. See, we both know that you're totally responsible for what happened to Heron. It was *me* who found him, remember.

LILI: Well, you know what they say; finders keepers.

MARK: At first I couldn't believe my eyes.

LILI: That's what comes of running around in my wood under a gibbous moon.

MARK: Yeah, but the moon came and went that night in the wavering mist. So as I was running through the trees, suddenly I pulled up short, 'cause I saw what I first thought was…well, some kinda apparition. It was like a… spectre swaying in the mist, and the mist seemed to bubble around it like…curdling milk. But a moment later a gust of wind blew the mist away. And then in the full glare of the moonlight, I knew it wasn't just a figment of my imagination.

LILI: Yes, the Old Moon can appear to be a hag-like crone. And then She is the harbinger of divination and death, and sometimes madness follows in Her Wake.

MARK: But how, in God's name, could you have just left Bobby Heron like that? *(Realising.)* Of course! You played on his masochism, didn't you? To get him to harm himself.

LILI: No, actually it was sadism that turned Herr Heron on.

MARK: If he was a sadist, then why did I discover him hanging there, like some…some…?

LILI: *(Finishing his thought.)* …Giant rotten apple, swaying in the night wind.

MARK: So you do admit *you* made him top himself.

LILI: When he came to me earlier that night, he was crimson with anger. But then he was perpetually wedded to uncontrollable fury. You see, like you, Mark, Herr Heron believed that women have their place. And you can guess where that place was – and is.

MARK: That's no reason for him to hang himself.

LILI: Again – like most men – he was consumed by hubris, and rapacious pride always comes before the longest fall.

MARK: Yeah, with a goddam noose at the end of it. But I still can't understand how *you* can have been the lover of one poor bastard who topped himself, and then you were also the lover of that other poor bozo, who went stark-staring crazy. And that all happened in less than eighteen months. Yet the cops still let you off scot-free. When, by rights, they should have locked you up forever, and thrown away the fucking key!

LILI: For once, you've got the adjective right. So now all you have to do is give me the noun, which is in your pocket, jangling with your small change.

MARK: There you go again. When you're not calling it 'little', you're calling it 'small'! God, I've a mind to beat you to a mushy pulp.

LILI: Yes, and that's exactly what the other two tried to do to me. And also it's why enough proved to be more than enough.

MARK: Yeah, but you still haven't explained how you made those poor bastards destroy themselves.

LILI: Like you – they were both self-proclaimed God-fearing men, so the very least they to could do was to atone to the Goddess for their sadistic, Dionysian frenzy.

MARK: Oh, not the goggling Goddess again!

LILI: Always and forever.

MARK: Oh c'mon, you don't fool me, Lili, banging on about the myth of the Triple Moon Goddess. Oh yeah, I know that way back when - some folk believe that most humans worshipped the Moon Goddess. But that was before everyone realised the error of their ways. And once they did, they stopped grovelling before the stupid Moon, and instead they all rightly started to worship the One True God, Jehovah.

LILI: Again you're so wrong, Mark. It was the Ancient Greeks who tried to replace the matriarch, Moon Goddess, with their patriarchal gods, Zeus and Apollo. And the Greeks believed that they had destroyed the Goddess by reducing her into the Nine Muses. Yet despite the plethora of male gods that the Greeks, Jews, Christians and Moslems have conjured up between them, the Triple Moon Goddess still reigns supreme for She continues to create life on earth. Because as even *you* must have noticed, Mark, only females can give birth. Well, *you* certainly can't, boyo. So it's always been *Mother* Nature. Never Father Nature. *(She waves her bag of cherries under his nose.)* Talking of which, are you sure you won't try one of Her erogenous cherries?

MARK: No! And stop bloody lecturing me.

LILI: *(Between eating her cherries.)* Then stop lusting to dominate *other* women's children. And, instead, come to terms with the feminine side of your own nature. Then perhaps there will be a remote chance that you will re-learn how to love, and to nurture.

MARK: 'Love and nurture'! Coming from *you*, Lili, with your godawful record. But then, of course, you haven't always called yourself 'Lili', have you?

LILI: *(Amused and savouring another cherry.)* Haven't I?

MARK takes a large tome off the bookshelf, and pulls one of the many markers out of the book. Then he jabs his finger at a selected page.

MARK: Mind, I'm surprised you don't call yourself; 'Lili the Filly' – 'cause whenever you carnally target a guy, you sashay your chassis like there's no tomorrow.

Using the stalk, LILI waves a cherry at him.

LILI: You should know. You're the one with the perpetually twitching groin.

MARK: But you're the succubus revenant, who first seduces, and then you devour your victim like a praying-fucking-mantis. *(He watches her eat the cherry.)* But that's not surprising when - according to the Early Semites …. *(Reading from the book.)* …the name 'Lili', like the name 'Lulu'; well, they both mean 'lasciviousness'.

LILI: *(Amused.)* Is that translated from the Yiddish or Arabic?

MARK: Yeah, and, what's more, you smartass, you also used to call yourself 'Lilitu', didn't you?

LILI: You tell me.

MARK: I'm telling you!

LILI: Next you'll be saying that I was the screech owl in Isaiah 34;14. Mind, that, of course, was only in the King James Version.

MARK: If you weren't the screech owl in Isaiah, how come you're so familiar with the chapter and verse?

LILI: Probably because I was a Mesopotamian storm demon at the time.

MARK: I'm glad you know all your history - Ardat Lili.

LILI: I was only half of 'Ardat Lili'.

MARK: Which half?

LILI: The 'lili' half, of course.

MARK: No, you were – and are – both frigging halves. 'Cause according to this… *(He jabs his finger at the book.)* …in Ancient Akkadian, 'ardat' is derived from 'ardatu', which means 'prostitute'.

LILI: Which is why *I'm* the *other* half, because 'ardat' also means 'unmarried, beautiful maiden'. And that is exactly how I intend to remain.

MARK: OK, OK, let's stick with the Mesopotamian succubus, Lamashtu, 'cause that's what you really are. See, 'Lamashtu' means 'seducer of men and drinker of their blood, with the power of seven witches.'

LILI: *(Laughing.)* Only seven? Anyway, how can I possibly be Lamashtu, when she is renowned for so many other dubious characteristics? Well, for starters, unlike Lamashtu, I don't have the head of a lioness, and I certainly haven't noticed either of my breasts being suckled by a pig and a dog simultaneously, and there's no way… *(Finishing her last cherry.)* …while I'm riding a proverbial donkey that I have a scorpion's tail scooting around my womb, with its head peeping out of my vulva.

MARK: Jesus God! If you're just Miss Innocent Cherry Pie, like you claim, then why are you so familiar with all this shit about these innumerable, demonic succubi?

LILI: Oh I'm fully aware that I'm not a Born Again, twice-published children's novelist like *you* are, Mark, and that I'm merely one of the lesser species; i.e., a woman. But despite these obvious and inordinate drawbacks, strangely enough I did learn to read. And so, latterly, I developed this penchant for studying what is erroneously called mythology.

MARK: OK, OK, let's cut to the chase. God said, 'Thou shalt not suffer a witch to live.'

LILI: Bingo!

MARK: What?

LILI: I was wondering when you'd finally come to the crux of yourself – Mr Hopkins. You see, it's not just me, who has a name to conjure with. And as you have read so much about *me*, undoubtedly you must have read all about *you*.

MARK: What's there to read about me? Hopkins is just Hopkins.

LILI: Will you never stop lying to yourself?

MARK: I'm not lying. The only thing vaguely interesting about my name is I share it with another Hopkins, who's done pretty well for himself. And that is, of course, *Sir* Anthony Hopkins.

LILI: Yes, but Sir Anthony never changed his name from 'Matt' to 'Mark' – like *you* did - Mr *Mat-thew* Hopkins.

MARK: I haven't changed my name, either!

LILI: And the reason you've changed your name is why I'm sitting here now, eating all these truth-invoking cherries in front of your sacrificial altar.

MARK: Only shitty pagans sacrifice people on altars! Like you and all those blinkered morons used to do, in homage to your so-called Triple Moon Goddess. And that's why the 'King' had to die annually, didn't he? To propitiate the Moon Goddess, in the vain hope that she'd shine down on good harvests for everyone next year. It's also why you and a bunch of your witches would lure some poor bozo down to the sea. Then you and your coven would make him climb high into a wickerbasket. And once the poor bastard was trussed up in the basket, you'd all set him alight at high tide under the Lammas moon, and gleefully watch your victim burn to death 'till he was just a smoking cinder.

LILI: I have never watched anyone burn, Matthew. At least not voluntarily. That's not the way of the Goddess, who commands us to love and create life, not to destroy it. No, *you* are the one who nightly dreams of all your victims being burnt alive.

MARK: Burning is certainly the fate *you* deserve, 'cause you're the Wicca-succubus, aren't you? *(LILI laughs.)* How can you laugh? It's not funny.

LILI: There's such a thing as sardonic laughter. Especially as it would take the lifetimes of two Molières to deal with all your hypocrisy.

MARK: Now don't duck the facts, Wicca-succubus. Oh I know very well that your 'Wicca' is in no way related to the 'wicker' tree, with its highly-combustible 'Wickerman'. No, no, your name is even spelt differently – 'cause yours is 'W' 'I' 'C' 'C' 'A' – as 'Wicca' is the Neo-Pagan word for 'Witchcraft', right? And that is why 'Thou shalt not suffer a witch to live.'

LILI: And, what's more, *you didn't* let them live, Mr Hopkins.

MARK: So for everyone's sake – and safety – Wicca-succubus, now you have to pay the price – in full - for all the evil you've perpetrated through the ages. *(He goes behind the altar. Then he lifts up the altar-cloth, and he pulls out a large canister.)* Yeah, I know - when I first came down here - this is what you were looking for, right?

LILI: I didn't have to look.

He advances on her with the canister.

MARK: Next you'll be telling that this doesn't scare you shitless.

LILI: Only a children's novelist could have such a telling way with words, Matthew.

MARK: Stop calling me that!

LILI: How can I? When 'Matthew' is your real name.

MARK: No, it's not. And you can quip all you like, bitch, 'cause your games are over now.

LILI: So you're willing to join me in the inferno, then?

MARK: No, your coming ordeal is for you, and you alone, baby.

LILI: Then this will be the first time that you will make your infernal dreams into a flaming reality – won't it, Mr Matthew Hopkins?

MARK: Why the devil d'you keep calling me that?

LILI: Because you are about to meet the Devil in person, Matthew Hopkins.

MARK: Again you're so wrong. The Devil's Inferno is where *you're* going – as a long-over-due punishment for all your Wicca-succubi crimes against humanity.

LILI shakes her head and laughs. In response MARK slams the white canister down on an adjacent chair.

LILI: Really? So how do you propose to send me there?

MARK: Like this! *(MARK runs across the room and grabs LILI by her hair, which is shoulder-length. With his other arm, he puts a strangle-hold around her throat, but she tries to fight her way free.)* No, no, this is a fait-accompli, you Satanic whore! So there's no point in you struggling.

LILI: *(Shrugging.)* Then how can I possibly resist such macho charm?

MARK Now you listen to me, you smartass malefica – yeah, I know my Latin – and now you listen good. 'Cause there's no way you're gonna trick me into topping myself, or driving me into the funny-farm, like you did with the other two.

LILI: Right. So what's next? Are you proposing to rape and pillage me, and then are you going to sacrifice me on your altar as your latest offering to good, old, beneficent Yahweh?

MARK: It's the very least you deserve.

LILI: There's nothing like a Born Again Christian for speaking his mind.

MARK: God, if only you didn't smell so sweet, you filthy little slut.

LILI: Which is more than can be said for you?

MARK: I don't have b.o.!

LILI: Violence has its own stench.

MARK: How can you make jokes when you're about to meet your Maker?

(MARK tightens his strangle-hold around LILI's throat.)

LILI: For pity's sake, Matthew…! *(Choking.)* I can't breathe… I can't…

(He exerts even more pressure on her windpipe.)

MARK: You don't deserve to breathe, you blood-sucking witch! Dying's too good for you.

LILI: *(In an exhausted whisper.)* Then the Goddess be praised, at last…it's all over.

(He continues to tighten his strangle-hold around her throat.)

MARK: Yeah, and now you'll see the Almighty face to face in Purgatory, where you'll answer for all you've done to every guy you've ever met. Then the Lord God will hurl you into the bowels of Hell! *(In response LILI gasps painfully, and suddenly she goes limp. MARK gives her neck a final jerk. Then he releases his hold on LILI, and she crumples onto the carpet at his feet. In disbelief MARK kneels beside her inert body.)* Oh c'mon, Lili, you don't fool me, you cunning bitch. You're just playing another of your frigging games. You're no more dead than I am. *(He seizes her motionless wrist.)* So where's your godforsaken pulse? Yeah, but knowing you, I bet ya don't even have one, do you? Though you must have! *(He presses his index finger on the inside of her wrist.)* So your pulse has gotta be… here. Or…here. But there's… nothing… Absolutely nothing! Yet when I … *(He flexes his hands around her throat.)* …well, you scarcely suffered at all, did you? And after everything you've done, that's so goddam unjust. *(Unsteadily he gets to his feet. Then he turns towards the altar.)* And I only did this for *You.* But it's never enough, is it? You always want more and more from me, 'till You've sucked me dry. *(Shaking his head in despair, he goes behind the altar. Then he pulls a bronze crucifix out from under the altar cloth.)* But then, of course, no one's ever understood suffering like You did… *(He places the crucifix between the flickering candles.)* …'cause You let Yourself be crucified, didn't You? So You're the first Holy Masochist. But You had one helluva reason to do what You did. Unlike me. *(In despair he puts his head in his hands.)* Oh Jesus, just listen to me. When I stopped drinking, I swore I'd never talk to myself again. Yet now I do nothing *but* talk to myself. And that's 'cause I'm the only person who listens to me. *(He addresses the crucifix.)* Well, I'm darn certain *You* don't listen anymore. That's why I've got no choice but to do what I'm gonna to do. *(He blows out the flickering candles on the altar. Then he throws the candles down beside LILI's body.)* See, if I *don't* do this, when the cops find her body, they'll sure as hell lock me up, and throw away the goddam key. *(Simultaneously he wraps up the crucifix and the empty candlesticks in the altar-cloth.)* And I couldn't bear being locked up in a cell for years and years... *(He places the altar-cloth-bundle beside the curtained cellar door.)* ...'cause then I'll be just like the rest of her victims. And she'll go on laughing at my suffering, ad infinitum, from her grave. So there's only one solution... *(Now chuckling to himself, he picks up the white canister.)* ...and that's to douse the bitch in petrol, and turn my cellar into her funeral pyre. 'Cause she's right, of course; I am always dreaming of burning. That's why the inside of my skull is perpetually on fire. But now she's gone, there's no one who can bring me any relief. *(He stands over LILI's body, and he is about to unscrew the cap off the petrol canister, when he shakes his head in sudden disbelief.)* No, no, it's not possible. The dead...can't breathe. *(He puts the canister down, and he kneels beside her body.)* It's just an illusion... Or did your eyelashes...really flicker? *(He touches LILI's face.)* They did. Let me see your goddam eyes. Right, then I'll force 'em open! *(With his forefingers and thumbs, he pulls back her eyelids.)* Nothing but...blue spirals... of nothing. *(In awe he whispers.)* Yes...looking into your eyes is like...peering into a double...abyss. *(He seems to be in a hypnotic trance.)* Your irises are drawing me in deeper... and deeper...down into the purgatorial fires of...the dead... But with your flames engulfing me, why do I feel... so very...very...sleepy...and spacey...?

LILI: Because you need to go into the depths of yourself, Matthew Hopkins, to confront the truth about yourself.

MARK: *(Now having great difficulty speaking.)* You're... hypnotising me...aren't you?

LILI: No. I have already done that, so it's pointless you trying to fight the inevitable.

MARK: What's...happening to me?

(LILI sits up. Then she crouches beside the immobile figure of MARK.)

LILI: Once again you are in the fateful year of 1646, at the height of the Civil War, and you are – as ever – Matthew Hopkins, that unsuccessful lawyer, who, with the Puritans' blessing, and in Jesus Christ's name, is solely responsible for condemning more women to be hanged for witchcraft in England than in the previous hundred years.

MARK: No!

LILI: Yes! Between 1642 and 1644, with the help of your malefic minions, you tortured 300 so-called witches in the Counties of Middlesex, Essex and East Anglia. And you put all these poor jibbering women on trial, and erroneously found them guilty of practising witchcraft. Then you applauded their subsequent hanging. Yet there was not one single man among them.

MARK: Why can't I move my arms or my…legs…or…?

LILI: The manacles you bound victims with, those spectral chains bind your limbs now. So you have no choice but to remember the sixty-eight women that you put to death in Bury St. Edmunds. Then in Chelmsford, you hanged nineteen women in a single day. Naturally you were well-paid for ridding the towns of all these totally-innocent women. And some of the younger women you rampantly lusted after. When they refused your lecherous advances, naturally you called them satanic Wicca succubi, and herded them off to the gallows. While others were just midwives, or they healed their neighbours with potions, so naturally you condemned them for having a pact with the Devil, and you tortured and killed them.

MARK: But that was…a whole…world ago.

LILI: And, worst of all, you hanged most of these hundreds of terrified souls just for the money. In the town of Stowmarket alone, they paid you twenty-three-witch-killing pounds. Which was inordinately generous, considering the average wage was only tuppance-ha'penny a day.

MARK: Mercy! Please, show me some mercy!

LILI: I will show you as much mercy as you showed them, Witchfinder General.

LILI picks up the petrol canister. Then she pours the contents of the canister over MARK's now-almost-inert body.

MARK: But you said you never…burnt anyone in the name of your…Triple Moon Goddess… Or was that just another of your endless lies, you godless succubus?

LILI: Oh I don't propose to strike a match. I don't need to.

MARK: Then how…?

LILI: You seem to have forgotten why you asked me to come here tonight.

MARK: I don't see what…

LILI: *(Overriding him.)* Yes, and whenever you've come round to my cottage to pay me, it's always been for the very same service.

MARK: No!

LILI: Yes, because every day of your so-called devotional life… *(She points to the altar.)* …to Him…has also been devoted to stoking the lustful and envious flames that continually burn and torture your rabid mind and heart, until you have no recourse but to explode into frenzied violence. And you are especially violent against women. As you have only too readily shown twice again tonight, with me as your potential victim. Well, you certainly showed no remorse when you believed that you had killed me. So now it's time for you to pay the penalty for all your impious crimes. What's more, I prophecy – that before the Triple Moon Goddess wanes in Her Heavens – the Hell flames, *within* you, will totally engulf you, so that you, and you alone, will induce your *own* immolation. Then you will watch yourself as you slowly burn yourself to death.

MARK: Impossible!

LILI: In this best and worst of all possible worlds, you will discover that nothing is impossible. You see, throughout history, there have been many incidents of self-combustion. But in your case, over the period of the next two hours, you will watch your own body burn progressively, and in the following horrific sequence. First; your calves will bubble and erupt until you are hoarse with screaming. Then your thighs and your hands, your torso and your forearms will boil like cauldrons of molten blood. Then your chest, your beard, your nose, and finally your eyes will incinerate and explode. *(She takes the basement key from his pocket.)* And then, rely on it, Matthew Hopkins, you will be only too grateful when Death devours the very little that is left...of your erupting flesh.

After slipping her bag over her shoulder, LILI moves to the basement door.

MARK: You...can't...leave me like this...

She pulls back the curtains that cover the basement door.

LILI: I'm only doing to you what you were proposing to do to me.

MARK: Oh God...already I feel the fire...rising inside me...

LILI: So there is such a thing as natural justice.

She unlocks the basement door.

MARK: Help me!

LILI: How can I? When I am – as you call me – merely the Wicca-succubus. *(She is now standing in the open doorway.)* While *you* are so much more important, because you are in the long and endless line of devout, self-cremating... Wicker-incubi. And in your case, 'Wicker' *is* spelt 'w' 'i' 'c' 'k' 'e' 'r'.

LILI draws the curtains, so that she is hidden behind them. MARK cries out in great pain.

MARK: God in Hell!

LILI: *(From behind the drawn curtain.)* Yes. That is certainly where you will find your god.

Then the basement door is slammed shut, and we hear LILI's echoing footsteps as she ascends the basement steps.

There is a spotlight on MARK's open-mouthed, anguished features. The image is reminiscent of Edvard Munch's iconic painting 'The Scream' as the darkness possesses MARK.

A moment later, the curtains swish open again, and LILI can be seen framed in the open doorway.

LILI: Arise, and create a new life for yourself.

MARK: *(In disbelief.)* You're going to free me, then?

LILI: Only you can do that.

MARK: But I don't…understand.

LILI: As I told you, women prefer to create, rather than to destroy. So, Mark, Mathew, Luke and John, try to emulate us for once. Because I will always be watching you… and your fires will only need a little stoking, and their conflagration will reach up to the Moon. So…good night. Learn to love. And then…fare forward, Voyager.

LILI goes. Fade on MARK, who continues to stare after her. Then he shakes his head, with the beginnings of a disbelieving, half smile…

The End.